FEARON EARLY CHILDHOOD LIBRARY

Please Don't Sit on the Kids

ALTERNATIVES TO PUNITIVE DISCIPLINE

Clare Cherry
Director, Congregation Emanu El Nursery School
and Primary Learning Center, San Bernardino, California

Photographs by Sam Cherry

Fearon Teacher Aids
A Division of Frank Schaffer Publications, Inc.

This Fearon Teacher Aids product was formerly manufactured and distributed by American Teaching Aids, Inc., a subsidiary of Silver Burdett Ginn, and is now manufactured and distributed by Frank Schaffer Publications, Inc. FEARON, FEARON TEACHER AIDS, and the FEARON balloon logo are marks used under license from Simon & Schuster, Inc.

Editorial director: Roberta Suid
Editor: Kate Fuller
Cover and text designer: Terry McGrath
Editorial production manager: Patricia Clappison

ISBN − 0 − 8224 − 5474 − 2

Library of Congress Catalog Card Number: 82-81981

Printed in the United States of America.

Contents

96227

Preface

This is a book about attitudes. We live in a society in which attitudes about the discipline of young children often border on abuse. The subject of discipline causes a great deal of confusion even among authorities. Punishment is the key word in our attempts to control children. We coerce. We negate. We threaten. We nag, produce guilt, and embarrass. We deprive. We isolate. And we physically abuse children (an action we excuse by calling it "spanking").

Although we readily excuse our own mistakes through rationalizations of one type or another, we seldom apply the same criteria to young children. Instead, we act towards them as though they deliberately go about the business of displeasing us. We don't acknowledge that they may be feeling nervous, harassed, anxious, fearful, jittery, lightheaded, confused, worried, excited, curious . . . or perhaps that they are hungry or have a headache. Rather we insist unreasonably that they must change their behavior to meet with our expectations and needs regardless of their feelings and capabilities.

There is just as much confusion in the school as there is in the home. This book is addressed to teachers of young children. It presents a system of nonpunitive attitudes which I have termed *Nondiscipline Discipline*. It offers alternative methods of intervention based on humane actions and rational communication. It is based on the simple concept that if we expect children to change their behavior, we must be willing to change our approach to that behavior. The term implies that our task is to help children learn to do right rather than to waste so much energy in stopping them from doing wrong. This book is written in the hope that, after reading and applying its principles, you will remember the phrase, "Please Don't Sit on the Kids," because, as my eight-year-old friend Sara said, "They just might not bounce back up."

One of the most pleasurable parts of writing a book such as this is the privilege of expressing one's appreciation to the many persons without whom its completion would not have been possible. I want therefore to thank my co-workers at Congregation Emanu El Nursery School and Primary Learning Center in San Bernardino, California, for evaluating my ideas with me and for demonstrating so skillfully that the magic list and the Nondiscipline Discipline methods do work. I want to thank my colleagues in the field of early childhood education and my students at California State University who have supported my efforts and assisted me in my research over the years. I want to give special thanks to Dr. Tennes Rosengren for his reading of the manuscript and his helpful suggestions; to Dr. Nikolai Khokhlov for his ongoing dialogues with me that were pertinent to the formation of many of the ideas; and to Sunny Wallick for the sharing of her time. And, though I haven't seen her for twenty years, I want to thank Dr. Martha Frank, my mentor, for her ongoing influence and inspiration, which have remained with me since she first employed me as a nursery school teacher. I also want to acknowledge the research done and the support and encouragement tendered me by my husband and partner, Sam. Thanks to him, too, for the photographs that compliment this book.

Clare Cherry

Dear Teacher;

I don't like to be disciplined. Do you? I don't like to be punished. Do you? I don't like to be "put in my place" or "straightened out for my own good." Do you? I don't like to be yelled at, pulled by my hair, shaken by my shoulders, or yanked by my arm. Do you? And I don't ever, ever, ever like to be spanked. Especially not by someone two or three times as big as me.

I want so much to be like you. I try so hard to do what is right and to make you notice the things I do. I try to remember all the rules, but there are so many. And sometimes I get nervous, or mixed up, or excited, or scared, and that makes me forget some of the rules. Then I get Trouble.

I really don't look for trouble. But sometimes you tell me to do something and I don't know exactly what it is you want me to do or when you want me to do it. And while I'm trying to figure it out, you get so mad that I get all upset and forget what it was you said in the first place. Then when I do the wrong thing, you get mad and nag and scold and make sure I notice my mistake. Then I really feel guilty and embarrassed and like I don't know anything, and it's no use to try to straighten things out because everybody is so excited, including me. And then I get mad at me.

What I really want, teacher, is for you to hold my hand and walk with me. Help me learn the things I need to know. Help me do right. I really want to. And help me to understand my feelings, because they're just like the kinds of feelings you have. And please, please teacher, don't just notice my mistakes. Please notice when I do something right.

I'm glad you're my friend. Please, teacher, keep on being my friend, and together we can grow.

I love you.

Child

Part I
DISCIPLINE: PROBLEMS OF CONTROL FOR CHILDREN AND ADULTS

Discipline from the Child's Point of View

1

Like all human beings, children need to receive love and to give it. Fulfillment of their physical needs alone will not ensure or maintain quality in their lives. Regardless of age, the inner self cries out for nurturing.

We adults, amidst the complexities and concerns of our own lives, often forget that children are individuals with feelings and thoughts of their own. We have our own plans and desires, among which are preconceived images of how our children will fit into our families, schools, and social systems. As we get caught up in the maelstrom of our daily lives, our children are, too often, just swept along.

For children to enter into and be accepted in the world of grownups is, at best, a difficult task. The addition of discipline and punishment to their lives adds to the stress of their struggle.

HOW CHILDREN SEE THINGS

Children have their own ways of describing their lives. To check my perceptions and to hear their ideas, I interviewed seventy-five children, ages four through eight. I asked each one, "What is it like being a child?" Following are some representative responses.

3

A girl, age six: *I like going to school, learning to write, going out to play and skating, riding the bus to school, and riding my bike. I would like to be seven years old. I don't like to be little, because then I can't be boss.*

A girl, age eight: *I'd rather be about thirty so I can be in charge.*

A boy, age six: *It's tough! Sometimes I'm forced to eat my cereal. Sometimes you have to get a spanking when you're a kid. Sometimes it's dumb being a kid because everybody thinks you're dumb. Sometimes it's great because grownups have to do all the work and kids get to have fun. The worst thing about being a kid is teachers won't ever listen to a kid.*

A boy, age five: *I would like to be very little so I could go into tiny places and someone can't find me when they're mad.*

A boy, age five: *Being a child is getting to play all day and don't have to do any work, and also since I am a child I don't have to watch my baby brother. But I have to watch him if they tell me to. I have to do what they tell me all the time. They always yell.*

A boy, age six and a half: *It's great because you get to do different things like going places or playing baseball. You don't have to worry about paying bills or going to work. Big people tell you what to do sometimes when you want to play.*

A girl, age five and a half: *I'm not a child. I'm in kindergarten. You learn about things, but sometimes the teacher gets too mad.*

A girl, age eight: *Boring. There's nothing to do because I can't do what I want to do. I wish I'd grow up tomorrow. I like to do the things my mom does, but I'm too little.*

A girl, age four and a half: *Children have to do what everyone tells them.*

A boy, age four and a half: *Sometimes children get spankings. That can hurt.*

A girl, age four and a half: *Sometimes children get spanked for nothing.*

A boy, age four and a half: *You get bossed a lot. The runaround system. 'Go ask your father.' 'Go ask your mother.' That's all I hear. And they yell a lot.*

A girl, age six: *Hand-me-down clothes. The oldest gets to go first. The youngest gets to be spoiled. I'm in the middle and I don't know what I get to do. But I get to play and eat hamburgers and ice cream. I like to go to school. I like to put my hands in paint. Grown-ups don't like that. They get mad. They want you to be clean all the time.*

A boy, age four and a half: *Children can't do everything they want to do. They're always being bossed around and forced to do things they don't want to do.*

A girl, age five: *You have more fun and learn things. But you get bossed. Sometimes they don't smile. But they love you.*

A boy, age five: *Big people can yell and push you around because you're just little and you can't grow up very fast. When you're left home with a baby sitter, you don't have much fun.*

A girl, age five: *Grown-ups get to go everywhere. Kids can't. Grown-ups decide for them. You can't do nothing.*

A boy, age seven: *Being a kid is hard when you have older sisters with boyfriends and your mom likes other people's boys, the way they act, better than you. She doesn't yell at them.*

A girl, age seven and a half: *The nicest thing about being a kid is what you do with parents when they are nice. But they're not always nice.*

A girl, age seven: *Being a kid is terrible. People are always telling you what to do. Sometimes they yell. Adults have no respect for you.*

A boy, age nine: *It's OK. But when your parents get a divorce you don't want to be a child. But I have fun, I guess.*

Overall, the children who were questioned seemed to appreciate childhood and the importance of play. Most of them seemed to know they are loved. But they also seemed to feel that there is a conspiracy by the adult world to prevent them from doing what they want to do when and how they want, and are best able, to do it. It seems obvious from the responses that children feel put down by, subservient to, and less significant than adults. Aside from play, the main themes running through the children's replies are desire for more control of their lives and feelings of fear and resentment toward angry, yelling adults.

CONTROL IN CHILDREN'S LIVES

Adult control of children's behavior begins with efforts to regulate basic natural functions, such as sleeping, eating, and toileting, during the first two years of life. These efforts often produce tensions and antagonisms that carry over into other areas of family life and erupt as conflict in minor incidents completely unrelated to these functions. Such conflict patterns may affect adults' attempts to regulate other developmental processes that children go through concurrently.

By age two, children begin to develop a sense of self. They pepper their language with loud, emphatic *no*s, challenging the control being exerted by their care givers. This sense of autonomy grows until, by the age of three, self-determination has become a key factor in children's lives. During the next two or three years, as the children's horizons widen, socialization becomes as important as self-determination. Children need to be able to experiment and explore to find out exactly what they can and cannot do and still remain within socially acceptable limits.

Gradually, as children reach the age of seven or eight, the need to control their own lives becomes an even greater force. They want to be able to choose things to do that interest them and that they do well. They want to avoid being made to do things they can't do well, things that create feelings of self-doubt and inadequacy.

With each new stage of development, the potential for conflict with the adult world is renewed. As teachers who work with young children, we must acknowledge this tremendous basic drive for control. We can create environments and develop systems of personal interaction in which children have legitimate opportunities to participate in the determination of the course of their own daily lives. We can develop attitudes within ourselves that convey to children, "I know you would like to be in control of your own life, but, for your health, safety, and growth, there will be times when we will need to work out those controls together."

When children know that they will be given options whenever possible, they will be more cooperative in situations that allow them no choice. They can be given options to exercise and develop their abilities to make choices. They can be included in decision-making discussions. They can be helped to develop the skills they need to make plans and follow through on them.

Children need encouragement from us—and lots of patience: It takes a long, long time to grow. In trying to help children grow toward independence, however, we often cause them—and ourselves—much stress. And in the eyes of the children, we often become angry, yelling adults.

ANGRY, YELLING ADULTS

Wittingly and unwittingly, we adults convey anger and disappointment to children in our most commonplace interactions with them. They are anxious to please adults and really want to do things right. Yet instead of giving children the support and encouragement they need, too often we reprimand them with put-downs and punishments. Indeed, there seems to be a growing trend toward stronger and stronger control over the behavior of children—by the use of positive as well as negative methods.

Today, adults suffer uncertainty, fear, and tension about the future. Until recently, American life followed a predictable pattern: school, job, marriage, home and family. Since the sixties, social upheaval, out-of-control inflation, and simplification of divorce procedures have created new patterns of living, mating, and child rearing. New anxieties have developed about drugs, sex, crime, and, more generally, unstable family life. Confused by shattered traditions and searching for immediate solutions, adults are caught up in the vicious circle of trying to change their children instead of changing the conditions that pose the real threat.

The conscious and unconscious anxieties that grip our society have created a condition of mistrust toward the future and toward our children's potential. We mistrust their—and our—abilities to cope with the rapid change that characterizes modern life. Lacking trust, adults deny children the opportunity to make choices freely and to learn of the many options that are available. Instead, children are faced with angry, yelling adults who slap, shake, threaten, and humiliate them. In today's schools? Yes.

Here are some comments I have heard from children discussing teachers: "She's mean." "She doesn't like me." "He's always yelling at somebody." "She grabbed me by the neck." "They make you feel dumb." "I think she doesn't like little kids." "They want you to be quiet, but they don't ever be quiet." "She makes you hurry and you can't do it right." "When I want him to help me he yells at me to sit down." "She slaps kids around." Pointing to shoulder: "He pulls my arm all the time and it hurts up here." "It scares me even when I know she isn't yelling at me." "Sometimes she doesn't ever smile. I guess she gets mad." "They won't say it again if you don't know what they said." "They always have problems and then get mad at you."

Children are very sensitive to even the most minor threat from a grown-up, even when it is directed at another child or the class as a whole. They see physical control as abusive and a raising of the voice as yelling and screaming, and they are especially concerned with unfairness and impatience.

WHAT DO THREATENING MEASURES ACCOMPLISH?

In discussing punitive discipline, I am not concerned with the person who has an occasional bad day and makes an occasional slip. I'm concerned with the common adult belief that it is all right to yell at kids, that it is all right to physically harass them, and that it is all right to hurt their feelings. Such methods are not all right; they are inhumane. They make children feel humiliated, overwhelmed, and powerless. Such methods instill fear, they make children feel like failures, and they fail my test of mutuality, or the Golden Rule of Awareness, which I define as:

"What I want for myself, I must also want for you; what I want from you I must also be willing to give."

While threatening measures may temporarily solve an immediate problem for a teacher, in no way do they improve children's behavior. On the contrary, they are a model for children of how to be an angry, yelling person who humiliates others. You'll find that the teachers who use these methods do so over and over again. If the methods were effective, they wouldn't need repeating. Children would learn more positive behavior. Instead, we have children who, having been made to feel that they are genuinely bad people, may act that way more.

Children usually will live up to and perform according to our expectations—even if the expectations are bad. Children who have been hurt and frightened badly enough may freeze up, lowering their own expectations of discovery and success, in order to stay out of the line of fire. Or they might do just the opposite. If they have been made to feel that the teacher is their enemy, they'll fight. That's what enemies do. They will imitate the harsh disciplinary behavior of their teachers both in their relationships with those teachers and in conflict with other children. Such conflicts will often be with children smaller and more helpless than themselves, again modeling the behavior demonstrated by their teachers.

Some children have enough self-esteem to withstand a teacher's irrational or immature behavior. They may obtain support from other adults or older siblings that is strong enough to counteract the deleterious effect of a nagging teacher. They may have so developed their powers of creativity and imagination that through dramatic play experiences they are able to work out the negative feelings instilled by the teacher and rediscover their own worth. If they have had help in learning to recognize their own emotional reactions and have achieved some control over them, they will be able to withstand the onslaughts of an overreacting teacher.

We tend to teach the way we have been taught. We tend to treat children the way we were treated as children. If we are caught in a pattern of hostile interactions with children that is tearing at our self-respect and self-confidence as professionals, or if we are having difficulty managing our own feelings, we need to reexamine our attitudes. Such patterns can be broken. We can effect changes—not only in ourselves, but in attitudes toward discipline of children in general. We can get away from the notion that it is all right for grown-ups to physically or verbally abuse persons who are one-half, one-third, or even one-fourth their size.

The years of childhood are brief. They should be years filled with wonder and the beautiful magic of play, of growing, of doing, of knowing. We need to listen to what children are saying. We need to give each fleeting moment serious consideration and know that we can help improve the quality of a child's life. We need to see children as the feeling, thinking, vital persons they are. We need to know them, to understand them. By doing so, we enrich our own lives.

Discipline from the Adult's Point of View

2 It is always an unfinished struggle to try to understand the points of view of children. We can give them life, live with them, learn with them, read about them, and keep up with all the current research about them, but we are still forced to interpret our findings from our own adult points of view. Our conclusions and interpretations are based partly on knowledge of what has already been found (by ourselves or by others) to be true, partly on what is taking place daily in our lives or jobs and with the children with whom we are involved, and partly on our personal beliefs. From these interpretations and conclusions come our hope or our despair for the future.

In spite of all of our studies and beliefs and intentions, we are still faced with some basic facts about child rearing: Young children need guidance to achieve self-direction, they need supervision to learn to live freely, and they need rules and limits to learn self-control. Their capacities for true autonomy, depending on their ages and rates of growth, are either latent, underdeveloped, or in the process of developing. We are the ones who must help them in this process. By our sensitive guidance and perceptive supervision, and with our innate awareness of their need for protection, we must help them learn the ways of becoming free, integrated individuals. We have the responsibility of guiding children toward the creation of a society that is more socially responsible and more reasonable than that which we know. We must model for children the enlightened use of our intelligence, the courage and strength to effect change, and the validity of caring for one another.

GOALS OF DISCIPLINE

The word *discipline* relates closely to the word *disciple*: It connotes that the person being disciplined is learning to emulate the person doing the disciplining. We need to examine the effects of any discipline we use as well as our motives in using it. If the real motive is to demonstrate our authority, superiority, and power, then discipline becomes more important than the people being disciplined. If we believe that learning can only occur through a strict system of rewards and punishment, then discipline becomes merely a system for filling children's minds with data.

We need to ask ourselves what children will ultimately learn from our use of discipline. Will they learn that children should be seen but not heard, follow but not lead, be informed but not think? Will they learn to value submissive, subservient, blind obedience to any authority for its own sake?

How can we teach children to evaluate and make choices, to be considerate and fair in solving problems with others? We need to ask ourselves if children should be punished for not yet knowing how to make wise judgments.

We need to be sure that we use humane methods of helpful discipline so that children may develop their own problem-solving and choice-making skills. Our aim must be to convey, through the disciplinary methods we use, such basic human values as respect, trust, honesty, and caring for others.

OUR MIXED EMOTIONS

The goals of a teacher are high; the responsibility is heavy. To get a perspective on how others handle the difficulties of this demanding profession, I interviewed many teachers. Here are some of their comments about their good and bad feelings in connection with classroom interactions with children:

"It feels rewarding. It's hard, fun, and frustrating. I worry about how rapidly the lives of little children are changing today. It's bewildering. Sometimes I want to cry."

"The parents have a lot of problems. I feel sorry for them. I feel a great sense of responsibility for the lives of the children during the time they are with me."

"There's almost a feeling of helplessness when I haven't been able to tune in to a particular person. It makes me wonder what's going on in that child's life and how I can break through."

"Sometimes, in spite of the joy, I become very nervous because I realize that so much of what I feel influences how the children will feel and react. I try to model a positive mood at all times, but some days are harder than others because I have some personal frustrations, too."

"Sometimes I feel very lonely. It's hard when you have nobody to share all the inner struggles — the successes and failures — in the day-to-day classroom situations."

"Although I greatly enjoy being a teacher, sometimes the responsibility becomes almost too overwhelming."

"I have good rapport with children. I see education as an exciting challenge. But I'm seriously thinking of quitting teaching because of the types of punishment for minor infractions my school is demanding of me."

"I have a lot of parents who seem to me to be too strict with their children. And their children are the hardest ones to deal with. I don't have enough opportunity to really get to know the parents and to try to help them see the normalcy of their children's behavior."

"It means a great deal to me. I really enjoy my rapport with the children. I get excited over each new step, each new achievement by a child. Financially it's very difficult. Many of my friends earn much more money than I do in other types of employment that require less education. But I seem to be healthier and more content with my life than they are."

"When I see how many things my children have in common, even though they represent different cultures and races, it's disturbing to realize how much the world stresses differences between people. Yes, teaching makes me feel a great sense of accomplishment, contribution, and success. But sometimes it gets discouraging. Some children are already so rude by the time they come to school, I end up wasting a lot of time trying to cope with their rudeness without becoming rude myself."

These teachers (and others I interviewed) expressed great personal pleasure and satisfaction at seeing learning occur— especially at making breakthroughs with late starters or slow learners. They all felt that teaching is hard work but very rewarding. Though they have a great deal of empathy for the parents of their students, they feel the parents do not appreciate the need for interaction with teachers. They expressed feelings of isolation and the need for some kind of support from other staff persons.

The teachers I spoke with were largely optimistic, and all seemed to have a fairly good sense of self-esteem. Though there was much enthusiasm, there were also strong underlying currents of despair. There was much concern about societal changes that are so greatly affecting children's lives and about the inability to make inroads in regard to institutional change— especially change in discipline.

The feelings of despair and helplessness were especially apparent when I raised the topic of discipline. Some teachers said that with so many more important concerns, and with so much learning and living and growing for the children to do, they wished the entire subject of discipline (commonly interpreted as "control of children") would just go away. Nonetheless, many of these teachers use humane methods of discipline and guidance and consciously try to avoid the fatal slip from influence to authoritarianism—from being one who facilitates learning to one who only "teaches and commands."

PERSONAL CONTROL

Teachers have such negative reactions to the subject of discipline because it raises questions for them about themselves as teachers. Discipline is something teachers feel they must resort to when things get out of hand—when they have lost personal control or control of the classroom. Losing control of themselves is of special concern because, in the process, many teachers lose sight of the goals of helpful discipline. Usually the anger-causing behavior of a child or several children is the catalyst for a teacher's losing personal control. Anger interferes with the teacher's judgment, and a lack of judgment in turn contributes to an already deteriorating classroom situation. Therefore, handling anger is the first method of maintaining personal control that a teacher should master.

Handling anger

To begin my search for ways to help, I asked the teachers I interviewed, "What do you do when you get angry?" Interestingly, most of them just looked at me for a moment or two. Quite a few said, "Angry? I don't know if I get angry." And then, as they began to think about it, they realized that they were falling into the common trap of denying their true feelings. Here are some of their comments:

"I tense up. I get a headache. Then I glare."

"I bite my lips and clench my teeth."

"I clench my fists. Sometimes I get so angry I actually take my fists and pound them on the table. If that doesn't help, I yell."

"Oh, I get all tied up in knots. My throat starts hurting. Then I start picking on someone. I always seem to need a scapegoat to alleviate my own guilt for losing control."

"First I talk in a loud whisper. And I glare. Then, I wait. Pretty soon, I talk louder—and louder. And I stare meaner and meaner. Then, if all else fails, I guess you can say I begin shouting."

"I get tense and nauseous. I always wish I could leave the room and go throw up. But instead, I release my feelings by taking it out on the kids—even the ones who weren't at fault."

"I start breathing hard. I take a big, deep breath or two. Then, if I'm still angry, I begin raising my voice."

"I count to ten . . . slowly . . . out loud. The kids soon learn that if they haven't quieted down or given me their attention by the time I reach ten, I really get mad. I yell, take away privileges, and create stupid punishments."

"I take a deep breath and count to ten. Then I explode."

"I get a headache and get very frustrated. I don't want to get angry. I might even walk out of the room for a moment. But I have to go right back, because I can't leave the kids alone. I wish I could. Maybe that's what they need—to be left alone for awhile. I know that's what I need."

"My shoulders get tense. I tighten up all over. I get a backache from trying to control myself. And, in spite of all that, I end up banging a book on my desk anyway . . . loudly."

It is obvious from their replies that even the most skilled teachers need to express anger when they feel it. Anger is a healthy, normal human emotion. We don't seek anger. Some occurrence takes place and our mind acts on it, frequently by developing a feeling of anger. It is important for us to realize that it is the mind that makes the decision, even when we think we are doing something automatically. This is the first stage of anger, the cognitive stage. We may not have an awareness of anger building up during this stage, but it is there nonetheless.

When we become angry we may also be expressing feelings from other aspects of our lives. For example, one person who sees children fighting may relate the fight to problems at home. Another person may feel guilty for not having taught the children better ways to work out a disagreement and become angry as a response to the guilt feelings. For yet another person, the fight may stimulate an unconscious memory of having been a meek, nonbelligerent child, a disappointment to his or her parents, and anger may stem from that old embarrassment. Whatever the incident, it is important to remember that, at the very onset of anger, it is the thought that counts.

Just as we are all unique individuals, so we are also part of the human family, sharing universal traits. Part of our commonality lies in our bodily functions. Anger, which originates in our mind and which we may or may not be aware of, causes certain physiological modifications to occur that, in turn, increase our excitement. This is the second stage of anger, the physiological stage. Our muscles become tense; increased respiration and accelerated blood flow may cause our faces and necks to become flushed; the hairs on our arms and on the backs of our necks may bristle, heightening the effect of the tightened muscles in those areas; perspiration increases. These physiological effects cannot be denied, and there may be other signs.

Prolonged suppression or repression of feelings can have adverse effects on both physical and mental health. Anger must be recognized and dealt with. I propose the following steps for learning to manage anger in a healthy, productive manner.

Develop cognitive awareness. Learn to recognize the first feeling of anger when it is still in the cognitive stage, before physiological reactions have begun to take place. For example, when you realize that you are becoming annoyed, try to limit that annoyance to the cognitive stage by figuring out why you feel annoyed. This is where self-awareness becomes important. Socrates stated more than two thousand years ago that you must know yourself before you can know others. If you honestly and sincerely want to expand your awareness, you will acknowledge major and peripheral annoyances in your out-of-school life that may be reflected in your quickness to anger in the classroom.

A good first step towards greater self-awareness is to keep a record of incidents in which you find yourself becoming angry. Combine this record with notes on your life in general. After three or four weeks, review your notes. You may discover clues to your hidden motivations, such as a connection to your personal life or your relationships with your employer, other staff members, or even the parents of your students. You may find a pattern that occurs at a particular time of day, month, or year. You may even be able to relate your anger to something as simple as hunger or fatigue.

Once you have acknowledged that cognitive first phase of anger, you can often manage to deal with it then and there. You may decide that the incident isn't really worth getting angry about. You may realize that it isn't the child or the class that you are angry at, but something in your personal life. You may realize that what the child or children are doing doesn't warrant anger—that the behavior is due to normal curiosity or a misunderstanding. When you can recognize the beginnings of anger, you can often manage to release the anger simply by stating, "I'm getting angry."

Develop physiological awareness. The second step in learning to control your anger instead of letting it control you is to become aware of your physical reactions. If you recognize certain physical reactions as signals that anger is occurring, you can use them to control the anger. For example, when you feel a part of your body becoming tense, recognize the tension and voluntarily increase it for an instant; then release it. This is the converse of denying or suppressing it. When you suppress tension, you activate other muscles in your body, usually muscles that are in opposition to—antagonistic to—the muscles that have already become tense. Antagonistic muscles create inner antagonism. Instead of biting your lips, gritting your teeth, or otherwise tightening your already tense body, you need to find a healthy way of releasing that tension. If you do not release angry tension, it escapes on its own. You see it when teachers shout, make insulting remarks, inflict unjust punishments, pick on the non-misbehaving children, and go to other extremes in order to "let off steam" or, as one teacher put it, "explode."

Express anger rationally. The third step in learning to handle anger is to realize that the expression of anger can be used legitimately and constructively.

IRRATIONAL EXPRESSION OF ANGER	RATIONAL EXPRESSION OF ANGER
• communicates only negative messages	• is a valid communication tool
• intensifies the anger in others	• lets others know how you feel
• replaces your anger with guilt, lowered self-esteem, humiliation, embarrassment, and other negative feelings	• relieves your own tensions and restores your emotional equilibrium

- degrades others by attacking their character, personality, family, or lack of skills
- models for children the irrational expression of anger

- does not reflect on the character or personality of the children or anyone else
- models for children ways they, too, can express anger in a rational manner

The rational expression of anger allows you to build and use an expanded vocabulary. In addition to saying "I'm getting angry," "I feel very angry," or "The noise is making me nervous; that makes me very angry," here are some alternative words you could choose:

aggravated	cross	furious	mad
agitated	disappointed	incensed	mortified
annoyed	dismayed	infuriated	offended
antagonized	displeased	irate	provoked
bristling	exasperated	irked	put out
bugged	fuming	irritated	sore

It's surprising how merely searching for a substitute for *mad* or *angry* can relegate the entire problem to the cognitive realm, where it belongs. Besides, finding alternative words for *angry* can become quite an interesting game. You and the children will find that "I'm really bugged" has a much different connotation than "I'm infuriated," and that "That irks me" is quite different from "I'm offended." The variety of these feeling-expressing words will gain the children's attention, and you'll be expanding their vocabulary as well. You'll know you've achieved something when a parent tells you that one of your students has cooled a fight with a sibling by saying, "Don't do that! I'm getting antagonized."

Once you've developed an "anger" vocabulary, the next thing is to practice saying things that tell how you feel without humiliating or degrading the children in any way. You always need to remember that children are learning, growing people. They don't deliberately want to make you angry. The advantage you have is that you deliberately want to express how you feel.

IRRATIONAL EXPRESSION OF ANGER	RATIONAL EXPRESSION OF ANGER
You make me angry. (The message is "You are in control of me, the teacher. You have the power to make me angry.")	*I feel angry.* (The message is a simple statement of how the teacher feels.)
You've ruined my whole day. You've upset the whole class. (The message is "You're not only bad, but you have power over the entire class as well as me.")	*I'm tired of asking you to stop that shrieking. The noise bugs me.* (The message is a simple statement of truth: The noise bothers the teacher, who is tired of asking the child to stop. It in no way demeans the child or the teacher.)
You kids make me so mad, I can't even think. You make me want to get out of here and just go home. (The message is "I am a weak person. You children are much stronger than I am. You can even drive me away from my job and my responsibilities.")	*When you kids don't follow directions, it really annoys me. Sometimes I get really irritated.* (The message states simply that when the children don't follow the teacher's directions, he or she gets annoyed and irritated. The teacher in no way relinquishes control.)
You are a disgusting, horrible child who doesn't care about anybody. (The message is "Keep on being disgusting and horrible because that is what I expect of you.")	*That kind of language offends me. It is inappropriate to use at school.* (The message is that offensive language is inappropriate to use at school.)
You dummy! Don't you know that could kill him? Don't you know any better? I give up with you. (The message is "You are an unworthy child who may as well stop trying to please me because I have given up on you.")	*Give me that shovel. I'm really annoyed. Tools need to be handled carefully. They are definitely not for hitting.* (The message is that using a tool as a weapon is inappropriate and makes the teacher angry.)

You stupid fools. Pick that up right now and don't you ever touch that science table again. (The message is, first, that the teacher thinks the children are stupid, so they may as well do other stupid things in the future, and second, that the teacher is a liar—they know they will use the science table again.)

This is the worst class I've ever had. How could you do that. I'm going to put all these books in this box and we won't have a single book in this room for one solid month. (The message is not only that the children are not expected to try to remember the school rules, because they're already so bad, but that books aren't very important—they aren't even needed in the classroom.)

That infuriates me. We keep this equipment on the science table for experiments, not on the floor to roll balls at. I'm so irked I don't even want to discuss it. (The message is that the teacher is very angry about the misuse of the equipment, but that there is no need to discuss it while being so angry. The message expresses trust that the children will put things back and not be so careless with them again.)

Seeing those books thrown over the floor really makes me mad. Books are our friends. Please put them where they belong right now. (The message is that books need to be handled with care, that the teacher is angry, and that the children are expected to put them where they belong.)

Notice that in the column for the rational expression of anger, the teacher is using "I" messages. "I" messages let the children know how the teacher feels, not how the teacher judges them or thinks they should feel. Throughout this book you will find numerous examples of "I" messages and other ways to express anger rationally.

Release tension outside the classroom. The last step in handling anger in a rational manner is releasing tension outside the classroom. Popular methods for doing this are yoga, meditation, dance exercise, and body building. Exercise is one of the healthiest and most natural ways of relieving stress. You can go walking, jogging, or running, alone or with other people. Rising early and going for a brisk walk or a short run before starting your working day can give you extra oxygen and raise your metabolism so that you start your day with energy. The invigoration brought about by exercise can carry over into all of your daily activities. Exercise works best if you do it on a regular basis—not necessarily every day, but you should try to do it at least three times a week.

You don't need to wait until you're away from work to relieve stress through physical exercise. If you've had an especially emotional morning and feel a lot of pent-up tension, go for a brisk walk before you sit down to eat your lunch. You'll be more relaxed and able to evaluate the morning's problem with greater clarity.

Hobbies have long been known for their recuperative effects. Hobbies such as gardening, carpentry, oil painting, or modeling with clay can greatly refresh the human spirit. As your eyes and hands get involved in an activity, many difficult problems may fall into their proper perspective. Anger dissipates and calm is restored. You should experiment and use the ways you find work best for you.

Don't despair if you lose control. In spite of your efforts to express your anger rationally, and in spite of your best intentions, there will probably be times when you will lose control. You'll find yourself shouting, berating a child for a real or imagined infraction, and meting out unfair punishment. It is better, I think, for a teacher to let his or her frailties occasionally come through than to act like an automaton. When you make a slip and "lose your cool," you can say to children, "I'm sorry I'm so upset and angry," or "I'm sorry that I shouted at you," or "I'm sorry I lost my temper." You can then say, "I'm not feeling angry anymore, so let's sit down together and discuss why it's wrong to throw rocks into the toilet." If you demonstrate the art of apology to the children, you will find that they will learn to give apologies appropriately.

Sometimes you may not quite have lost total control, but you do feel your anger building up. This is a good opportunity to model positive management of anger by saying, "I'm too annoyed to talk right now. But I know I won't be so angry later on. I'll wait until I don't feel so cross. Then we can talk about what you just did." Again, modeling such behavior can teach children to wait until their anger is lessened before trying to settle differences.

Minimizing stress

Learning to express anger is but one of many areas of concern when approaching discipline from the teacher's point of view. There are many stresses that teachers have to handle besides anger-causing behavior. People come into teaching with high ideals. They start out with their newly received credentials, fresh plan books and curriculum guides, and nicely sharpened pencils. They get acquainted with their students and commence being a teacher. Soon they are overwhelmed by their high ideals, which often become the source of many of their frustrations. The techniques they learned, the games, the songs, the styles, the ideas — all failed to prepare them for certain salient facts:

• They are greatly outnumbered.
• The children by whom they are outnumbered are amazingly different from one another and from the ones they studied about.
• The teacher is expected to maintain an atmosphere of civilized cooperation, academic pursuit (or, for younger children, the pursuit of preacademic skills), order, and logic, when sometimes it seems as if all the children are agitating toward chaos.
• The children have to learn to adapt to the teachers' expectations for socialization, even though they may not yet have acquired the skills to do so.

The great bulk of the responsibility is the teacher's, not the children's. Therefore it is important that you keep yourself in as good mental and physical shape as possible. That in itself can make the job of teaching and the problem of maintaining an ordered community within the classroom more pleasurable. In addition to taking care of yourself by expressing anger and relieving tension brought about by anger, there are other stresses which must be acknowledged, assessed, and dealt with. There are several steps you can take to assess your emotional and professional needs.

Keeping records. As mentioned earlier, record keeping can be very helpful in the development of self-awareness. It can help to identify patterns in your life and in your behavior (and in that of others) which may be causing problems. Two main advantages of keeping records are (1) you may be able to identify and dispose of many minor irritants before they become major ones, and (2) you can isolate irritants and take one problem at a time.

Sharing. Plan time between classes, during relief breaks or lunch periods, and out of school for sharing feelings and ideas with other teachers. These sharing sessions can be most productive when they concentrate on "I" messages and problem solving rather than complaints and fruitless gossip.

Managing time. Plan your time carefully. Try using a date book to keep track of appointments, errands, and other daily responsibilities outside of work. Allow yourself some personal time. Limit phone conversations to a reasonable, nontiring length. Try to handle papers only once; answer mail the day it arrives. Handling mail and other paperwork can also be facilitated by a large wastebasket.

Choosing priorities. Evaluate your obligations and try to eliminate those that aren't important. Put your time and effort into the things in your life that matter to you—things that have real meaning for your personal and professional well-being.

Planning short vacations. Even a day spent visiting another community can be a mental refresher, as long as you have planned your timing so as to avoid overexertion. Many "overnighters" throughout the year can make the need for long vacations less crucial.

Getting plenty of rest. Teaching is strenuous. Plan your days so that there is appropriate time for rest and relaxation.

Pursuing hobbies. As mentioned earlier, the pursuit of a hobby, especially one removed from the teaching profession, can greatly extend your personal resources.

Knowing your limitations. No one can be all things to all people. Know your own limitations and concentrate on doing well within them rather than extending yourself until you damage your mental and physical health.

CLASSROOM CONTROL

While bringing your personal and professional lives into balance is important, it is also essential to evaluate your classroom situation. Don't be afraid to turn things upside down and approach your classroom from some new angles. Sometimes it helps to "get off the freeway and take some winding country roads." Find out what your students need and how you can help them. You may find that you need to make changes in your curriculum and in your environment.

Balancing the environment

In classrooms where there is an excessive amount of misbehavior, aggression, and negativism, one thing is certain: We cannot change who the children are. But we can change our methods of coping with and responding to one another. We can also change the environment to give it a welcoming and relaxing atmosphere. We can take stress into account and deal with it by developing a stress-reduction program as part of the ongoing curriculum.

Physical environment. The classroom should welcome children by its initial appearance and comfortable arrangement. The children should experience a feeling of harmony and acceptance upon entering.

Your answers to the following questions can help you evaluate the atmosphere of your classroom:

- Is the color scheme interesting yet restful? Intense colors may elicit overactivity, dark colors may be depressing. Subdued colors are most conducive to cooperative behavior.
- Is the lighting adequate but not so intense as to be overstimulating? Fluorescent lighting can cause hyperactive behavior in some children. A good lighting plan is one that is changeable, allowing the lights to be subdued. This can have an instant calming effect during periods of overexcitement or overstimulation.
- Are the air conditioning, ventilation, heating, and humidity healthful and comfortable? Too much heat in hot weather and too little in cold weather can be irritating to children and adults alike, thus causing changes in behavior. Very high humidity can cause headaches; too much dryness can cause lethargy; too poor a flow of oxygen can cause drowsiness and depression. Any of these conditions can lead to poor behavioral activity and lack of normal response.
- Are the acoustics such that there are excessive reverberations of outside or inside noise? Children who evidence much hyperactive behavior are often unduly sensitive to sounds. Reverberations can be both annoying and stress promoting. Reducing the noise level frequently results in a decrease in hyperactivity.
- Are play areas and study places attractive and orderly? When play or study areas are accessible and comfortable, children are more apt to be careful and orderly.
- Are things always exactly the same from month to month, or does the environment undergo constant small, interesting changes? Small changes, such as a new picture, a change in the placement of a table, a rearrangement of a study area or housekeeping space, or a new plant acknowledge our continuously changing world.

Learning environment. The curriculum should make children feel capable, comfortable, and appropriately challenged. Answer the following questions to evaluate your curriculum:

• Are choices available to suit each individual's interests, capabilities, and needs, both developmentally and educationally? Are such choices presented democratically? When the curriculum is interwoven with choice making, children are automatically given experience in controlling what they are doing and when. This negates many of their urges for misbehavior that arise to satisfy their innate need to be in control. Choices are often reserved for the gifted and most well behaved children. *All* children need experience in making choices for their individual personal growth.

• Are time blocks structured for those who need to move and work fast as well as for those who are slower paced? We operate on individual rhythms. Classrooms that give cognizance to this fact allow for self-pacing of many activities, which in turn leads to more cooperation and wholesome response on the part of the children.

• Do lively activities alternate with sedentary activities throughout the school day? To prevent boredom, fatigue, overstimulation, or lethargy, the human body needs changes of pace and activity throughout the normal day. Providing this can prevent, or at least minimize, many of the common behavior problems of children.

• Is there a stress-reduction program in your school? Within such a program, the staff takes steps to deal with societal pressures, family problems, and everyday tensions that can greatly affect the way children conduct themselves in group situations and at individual tasks. Children need opportunities to talk about their worries, their concepts of what is happening in their homes and in the world, and their fears and feelings. For a complete guide to a stress-reduction program, see my book *Think of Something Quiet*, Pitman Learning, 1981.

Other environmental influences. Other areas you may want to examine are:

• provisions for rest, nutrition, and free time
• provisions for unusual weather
• provisions for parents' participation in school programs

or in meeting with staff and other parents
• approaches to competition among the children both aca-
demically and in sports activities ("Let's see who can be the
first one finished" as opposed to "I want you to try to get the
answers correct, so take your time and read each one over
before you go to the next.")
• opportunities for the creative use of materials and ideas as
opposed to preplanned projects
• provisions for encouragement of imagination and inven-
tiveness

The type of environment that children are brought into can
directly affect their behavior. This is not to say that a pleasant,
wholesome environment will *eliminate* behavior problems, but it
does mean that some contributing factors will be reduced to the
degree that you can give your attention to more serious causes.

References to classroom environment come up throughout
this book. Look for them and consider how you can make small
changes in your own classroom — to your own and your students'
benefit.

Establishing trust and sincerity

Once you have assessed your personal needs and have reevalu-
ated and modified your classroom environment, you are ready to
concentrate on enhancement of the personal relationships you
have with your co-workers and the children in your classroom.
Trust and sincerity are the cornerstones of the approach I am
suggesting; they become the catalysts for change.

Children learn at a very young age to mistrust most adults.
By the time they enter preschool many children have been
tricked, coerced, and cheated by adults. They have been bribed
with rewards that were not given and promises that were never
kept. They have developed a feeling that it is safer not to trust
than to be fooled once again. They have learned that adults, not
always meaning what they say, use little subterfuges and double
talk in the hope that children will be confused and not recognize
their insincerity. In the minds of children, adults give mixed
messages, and sometimes they're just wrong. They say things are

easy when they're really hard. They say "You can do it" when the children know they can't.

How do you build trust in children who have developed mistrust? The first step is to show that you are going to trust them. Trust breeds trust. Start out with little things: "I trust you to put the puzzle back when you're through with it"; "I trust you to hang up your coat"; "I trust you to take only one cracker when the picture on the sign shows only one cracker."

It takes courage to trust. We're so used to controlling children by threats and *ifs* that it is, for many, a complete turnabout to place faith in a child. You can do so, however, if you show them continuously that they can trust you: They can trust you to be in the classroom when you're supposed to; they can trust you to give help when help is needed; they can trust you to so involve yourself with what they are doing that, by your presence and your awareness, you protect them from losing control of their actions or their emotions. They need to be able to trust you to empathize when they are crying, but not to probe and compound the issue by making them recount what has happened. They need to be able to trust you to allow them to fail, to give encouragement when they want to try again, and to give recognition when they finally succeed.

Teachers must be careful not to make promises that they may not be able to keep, and they must always keep the promises they make. If an emergency or unforeseen circumstance prevents you from keeping a promise on occasion, acknowledge that fact and apologize for it. By the tone of your voice, your expression, and your gestures and posture, you will impart sincerity and honesty, thus sustaining and increasing mutual trust.

As you establish an atmosphere of trust and sincerity, you can build on the warm mutual feelings that develop in the classroom. In an atmosphere of trust, children will explore their own individualities. They will not be afraid to be creative or innovative. They will develop awareness of their own uniqueness while appreciating the unity of the group.

A trusting climate is one in which there are rules for guidance and supervision. Young children need your help and protection; they need the security of knowing that you will set and maintain limits. But a trusting climate is also one that is open, honest, and caring. Attitudes are positive; the feelings of others are important. Trust and sincerity are demonstrated by both verbal and nonverbal communication.

Communicating politely

Here are some general rules of good communication which should be followed when interacting with children:

* Always be sure you have the attention of the child or children to whom you are speaking.
* Say exactly what you mean, using words that are appropriate to the age and understanding of the child. Enunciate clearly.
* Speak slowly and with patience. Modulate your voice so that it is low and gentle.
* Solicit verbal feedback and look for nonverbal feedback. Don't go on until you're sure that what you said was comprehended.
* Listen to what children say to you. If you don't understand them, help them to clarify it for you by repeating or rephrasing what they said. Don't rush them. Give encouragement. Reserve your response until you are sure you understand their intent.
* Don't be judgmental. Don't base your response on predetermined conclusions, but rather on what is said to you at the time.
* Touching is an important form of communication, especially with children. A gentle touch while you are speaking adds emphasis and improves children's ability to recall what you say.
* Other types of nonverbal messages are also important, since nonverbal messages make up 93 percent of all communication between humans. Your demeanor and expressions should match your words so that you don't give conflicting messages. Nod. Smile. Lean toward the child slightly. Look directly into his or her face. Attend — don't let your attention wander.

• Always speak to children as though they were your guests. That way, you just can't go wrong.

Good communication is demonstrated in the many examples given in this book. The principle is that what is being said and how it is being said — not the exact wording — is important. Take note of this principle and practice your own natural ways of communicating messages. Try to sound assertive without being domineering or authoritarian. Here are some tips for ways to practice getting your messages across:

• Practice talking out loud to yourself in the mirror at home.
• Tape-record yourself in the classroom; later, evaluate yourself in privacy.
• Role-play communication with other staff members. Try taking both the teacher's role and the child's role. This will help you evaluate whether you are really communicating your message.
• Learn to differentiate between sounding authoritarian and being authoritative. Children respect teachers who are firm, knowledgeable, and assertive — as long as they are also kind, polite, and understanding.

Communication is largely a matter of feelings. When relating communication to discipline and classroom behavior, think in terms of how each child may be feeling at a given moment, rather than what kind of action the child is performing.

Remember that by using "I" messages, you can let children know how you feel about a situation without stifling their messages about how they feel. Don't try to *tell* them how they feel; open the door for them to communicate with you. Help them expand their vocabulary for expressing feelings by your own use of varied, accurate terms. Avoid ambiguous words, such as "upset," which might really mean worried, embarrassed, impatient, frightened, or angry. Don't settle for saying you feel "good" when you really mean enthusiastic, challenged, relaxed, cooperative, festive, amused, or loyal. Striving for accuracy conveys your own honesty as well as your respect for your listeners.

In addition to talking about your own and your students' feelings, learn to discuss the feelings of characters in traditional stories. For example, in telling stories such as "The Three Bears," talk about the various feelings that are experienced by each character in the story as the story progresses. Gradually, as your students are able to identify more and more different kinds of feelings, you can demonstrate that it is possible to be in control of feelings instead of being controlled by them. You can model the use of deliberate responses to specific feelings as opposed to reactive, emotional responses.

Reconsidering the Ways
Children Irritate Adults

3 In struggling to develop independence, in wanting greater control over their own lives, in wanting people not to be angry with them, and in wanting to be acknowledged, children encounter great frustration. Their ways of expressing that frustration are often irritating to adults. Misbehavior by children and the resulting exasperation of adults are nothing new. A few years ago, I conducted a study in which I asked more than one hundred adults between the ages of eighteen and seventy-five what they remembered as the most common reasons for being punished, both at home and at school, when they were children (Cherry, 1979).* I compared my results to those of similar studies of the same question (Sears, 1957; Stolz, 1967).** More recently, I surveyed teachers of young children on the same topic. The results of these four inquiries were amazingly similar. I assembled them into the general categories of misbehavior, described in the following pages.

---

*Cherry, Clare. *Trends in the Use of Behavioral Control Methods by Parents of Young Children.* Redlands, California: University of Redlands, 1979.

**Sears, R., Maccoby, E., and Levin, H. *Patterns of Child Rearing.* Stanford, California: Stanford University Press, 1957.

Stolz, L. M. *Influences on Parent Behavior.* Stanford, California: Stanford University Press, 1967.

Disobeying rules

Disobeying rules includes not sharing, not taking turns, not following directions, and otherwise not responding socially as an adult would. Sharing and taking turns are social skills that children have to learn. One reason children attend school is to experience social contact and to explore social mores. They need guidance and practice to become socially skilled.

Not following directions is a very common cause of conflict. Adults become exasperated when they find that children are oblivious to instruction. If directions were limited to selected important tasks, however, children might not tune them out so easily.

While walking down a school hallway one day, I recorded directions that I heard being given to children, ages two and a half through seven, in two classrooms. This is what I heard in a four-minute period:

Hang up your coat. Close the door. Come over here. Sit down. Be quiet. Speak up. Do it again. Put it away. Take this to the table. Pick that up off the floor. Put that on the bulletin board. Don't drag the chair. Open your book to where you left off. Be careful. That's Jenny's; find your own. Don't run. Watch out. Wait your turn. Move back to your own place. Pay attention.

Adults do have a way of going on and on. It's small wonder that children feel subservient to us. We communicate to them in ways that are degrading, unfeeling, and dehumanizing. How would you like to enter a room and have another adult greet you with "Come in, close the door, wipe your feet, don't slam the door, hang up your coat, wait over there, I'll be there in a moment, come over here, take this book and find a seat"? Not exactly rude, but a little overwhelming. Yet in the onrush of our daily busyness, we often speak this way to children.

Also, we often don't communicate directions clearly to children. Then we become angry because they don't respond. Sometimes our communication is clear, but their perception is not.

There are so many reasons why, in their developing years, remembering and following directions is hard for children, even when they want to obey. Our task, then, becomes one of helping them to develop good habits of listening and responding while simultaneously developing our own good habits of listening and communicating.

Talking back and other forms of defiance

Defiance comes when children are out of control. Defiant children need firm, compassionate help in regaining control. Clear, explicit requests, given with respect and geared to the age of the child, will be accepted by children more cooperatively than will demands that are shouted out in a domineering, authoritarian manner.

Disagreements may warrant discussion, but don't mistake an argument for a discussion. Arguments are confrontations in which people express opinions and feelings but don't listen to each other. They are, by and large, a waste of time. Discussions, on the other hand, are a valid means of communication. You can simply refuse to argue, and you can teach children to discuss their problems.

Fighting and other forms of violence

Most children learn to use physical force by seeing others use it and by having it used on them by adults. Children generally do not want to hurt others. When young children use physical force, it is usually done without thought and probably without malice. Children respond well to being given alternatives. Discussions can be encouraged. With children who are too young to carry on discussions, the teacher can simply state the facts. For example, you might say, "You can stop hitting Tommy right now. He doesn't like to be hit. If you need to touch Tommy, touch him softly." Rather than simply saying, "Keep your hands to yourself," you can encourage gentle contact.

Being disorderly

I was one of those messy kids. No amount of nagging or coercion by my parents or my teachers seemed to change my habits. Yet I could be quite orderly when given no choice, and so can the children I've known. When things need to be picked up, or cleaned up, or put in a particular order, I say exactly what is to be done and when. For example, "Kristy, put the puzzle back on the shelf now," or "Before you come to get your snack, the toys in the playhouse need to be put away."

Adults must be very careful not to apply double standards when expecting neatness. I have seen teachers insist that children straighten out their play areas and the materials with which they have been working while the teacher's own desk and work counter were disorderly. Orderliness in the environment should be the responsibility of all the people using that environment, not just an isolated few.

Not coming when called

Children will come when you call them if they know you mean it. You may be telling them that you really don't except them to respond until your fourth and fifth call when you finally shout, "I said right now!" (even though you didn't really say it until then).

The method I've found to be successful is to say the very first time, "You may all come with me right now." If Johnnie doesn't budge, say, "Johnnie, I called you." Actually, he may have heard you the first time but it didn't register. A reminder helps him hear and respond.

I frequently give a choice by saying, "I want you to come here right now. You may come by yourself or I can bring you." Because I have already demonstrated that I follow through with what I say, the child usually chooses to come to me. I never give choices unless the alternatives really are acceptable, and I never use choices as threats. If I take the child by the hand, I do it gently but with sureness. I don't wish to hurt the child or to demonstrate anger. I simply want to be sure that the child comes with me. I am confident that the next time, the child will choose to come without my extra help.

Courting danger

When a child's safety is at risk, the first rule is to remove the child from the danger as quickly as possible. Don't worry at the time about right or wrong handling. Don't stand on ceremony—act. Children who repeatedly expose themselves to danger are probably in great need of an extraordinary amount of adult attention. Try extra hugs and loving touches. Become the child's friend. It may be that at home the child is willing to risk even death in order to get too-busy adults to pay attention to him or her. This carries over to the school, and the child is again willing to be at risk, having found out it is a good way to get adult attention. Let these children know that they are important to you and that they don't have to take risks to obtain attention. You can't tell them these things; you must demonstrate them over and over again.

Set firm limits on specific risks. For example, you can say, "You may absolutely not touch that switch at any time," or "Get down from that roof right now! I'm not allowed to let children up there." These things should be said with emphasis, but not as angry threats.

Using vulgar language

Young children enjoy experimenting with words, and such experimentation should be encouraged. But sometimes they begin experimenting with words related to toileting and sex. With two- and three-year-olds this can be ignored: If the words don't elicit shock, the behavior won't be reinforced. With four- and five-year-olds you can give explicit instructions: "Those are not school words. You may not use those words at this school at any time."

Sometimes children will start insulting one another and exploring the use of many vulgar words and phrases. This can be a time to sit down with the children and discuss openly which words are acceptable at school and which are so unpleasant (hurting words) that they may not be used. Children are sensitive to shock reactions and will go to extremes to get a reaction. Firm, precise rules about what they can and cannot say are all that is necessary. Avoid reinforcing the undesirable language through nagging and punishment.

Inappropriate sexual exploration

Children's curiosity about one another's sexual organs is natural. There are several ways of handling such situations in school. With two- or three-year-olds, you can usually ignore their actions: If you don't overreact, this type of behavior usually stops. With four- to eight-year-olds, you can say, clearly and without excitement, "At this school, you may not touch each other's vagina or penis"; or "At this school, you may not take off your pants in front of each other." If the message is given clearly, it will be received clearly. Avoid nagging, telling parents, or branding children as sexual deviates. Instead, monitor bathrooms, clearly express expectations to the children, and avoid making them feel guilty and that body parts are dirty. With children age seven and over, I have found that sex education classes totally eliminate the inappropriate use of sexually oriented words and inferences.

Lying and stealing

Preschool children have vivid imaginations and love to play make-believe. They frequently have difficulty differentiating between reality and fantasy and may need help in doing so. Sometimes children seem to be telling outright lies when in fact they are merely distorting: Because they are young, they misunderstand what really takes place.

Sometimes lying is deliberate. It may be prompted by fear of punishment based on past events. As children get a little older, they'll frequently get in the habit of lying to build their own egos, to make others feel jealous, to avoid punishment, or to gain adult attention. Whatever their reasons, children should be confronted with their lies unobtrusively to avoid embarrassment and should be encouraged to practice telling the truth. Unfortunately, children are given many examples of "little white lies" by adults. When adults model such behavior, children see that it is apparently all right to lie. Teachers need to be especially careful not to model such behavior.

Children sometimes develop a habit of taking things that belong to others. With such children, you can simply say, "That does not belong to you. You may put it back (or give it back) now." Sometimes children who are obsessed with taking things furtively or who lie frequently need professional help to get at the root cause of the obsession. (See Nondiscipline Discipline Problem-Solving Systems, pages 167–173.)

Tattling

Some children acquire the habit of tattling when their own self-esteem has been diminished, when their wrongdoings have been pointed out over and over, and when they have not been given constructive guidance toward more acceptable behavior. I have learned to handle tattling in a way that I feel helps children to learn new behaviors. When a child comes to me complaining, "Jeremy took all the best crayons and left us all the broken ones," I may say, "That's not right for Jeremy to do. But let's think of something that Jeremy does do really well. Can you think of something?" If the child hesitates, I may continue "How about the way he can climb the tree faster than anyone?" The child might respond, "Yeah. He throws good, too." Thus, while acknowledging Jeremy's wrong actions, the discussion ends on a positive note, and tattling is not reinforced.

Whining

Whining, I have found, is one of the most out-of-proportion irritants to adults, and yet it is one of the simplest to handle. Whining develops into a habit because it gets attention. Sometimes it becomes a major issue with a particular child. You can take care of whining very simply by refusing to respond to it. If the child is not ill or becoming ill, if the child is not suffering from a speech impediment or other physical handicap that may affect the way he or she talks, and if the child's basic needs are being met, you can just tell the child in simple language that you will not respond to whining. For example, you can say, "I can't understand you unless you talk to me." Most children will then stop whining. In extreme cases you can say, "You may go whine in the other room. I don't want to listen to it."

Doing schoolwork carelessly

When children are careless about their homework, teachers should not overreact. Teachers can anticipate the problem and remind both parents and children about homework by using a work calendar. Calendars can be made up for an entire month and assignments written in as they are given. Either the children or their parents can be required to fill in the time at which the work is completed.

Parents are more likely to cooperate when homework is not "busy work," but a meaningful extension of classroom studies. From time to time you may want to send notes home to parents that explain the purpose of the homework, suggest times for accomplishing it, and thank them for their support.

When work is sloppy, the natural consequence should be simply having to do it over. Punishment should not be connected with it. Your goal should be to help children take pride in the neat appearance of their papers. Therefore, if a student has to copy an assignment over, be sure that you allow enough time — not time during a recess or lunch hour.

Children who continually turn in sloppy work may be suffering from a visual problem, poor eye-hand coordination, or other perceptual difficulties. Many children with mild perceptual problems are very sloppy in their work because they have difficulty judging the pressure of the pen or pencil or even the pressure of their own hands on the paper. They may have difficulty assessing spatial relationships. Such children should be carefully evaluated for cause and then be given appropriate help.

Some children may work better in a bright light; others may have to be shown a posture that makes writing more fluid. Some children may need wider lines, a lighter pencil, or a finer pen point; others may need to be shown how to write more slowly. Whatever the child's individual problem, look for ways you can help, rather than becoming angry over a messy paper.

Not participating

Some teachers of elementary school children become angry at children who hesitate or refuse to participate. Rather than becoming annoyed, teachers may be able to help if they find out what the problem is. Are the children shy? Do they feel that if they participate they will make fools of themselves because they don't know the subject well or because they don't speak well? Do they want to participate but suffer from stage fright? Are they truly afraid? Have they been conditioned not to speak up when adults are speaking? Can they hear and understand well? Can they see the chalkboard clearly?

Many years ago I heard a story of a Mexican American girl who was quite bright in her written work. When questions were asked in class, she was always the first to raise her hand, but when called upon would never answer. The teacher would then call on someone else. One day, seeing the child alone on the playground, the teacher began a conversation with her. Finding that she had no trouble conversing with him, he asked her, "Why is it that here on the playground you talk with me, but in the classroom, when I ask you to answer a question, you never talk?" The child thought quietly for a moment and then said, "Well, when you ask the question, I know the answer. But to tell it to you I first have to say the answer to myself in my language, then translate that answer into your language, and then I can say it out loud. But by then, you have always called on someone else."

Children who do not participate in class need your help in learning to speak in front of others. Try working with small groups of five or six, with each child taking a turn to speak. Gradually enlarge the group to ten or eleven children, then to as many as fifteen or sixteen. Allow practice time for each newly enlarged group so as not to undo progress that has been made.

Some children may need help in thinking of something to say. A caring teacher will know enough about each child in a classroom to draw out a child by leading him or her to talk about a special interest or an unusual family event or other happening in the child's life.

Other factors to be examined are health, relationships with other children, and even so simple a thing as clothing. A child who feels that he or she is not very well dressed might be reluctant to participate in classroom activities. Whatever the problem, your job is to try to unearth it.

Reconsidering Why Children Misbehave

4 When we try to understand why the children in our classrooms misbehave, we often need to look past their behavior to factors beyond their control. Particularly when a child continuously provokes discipline or punishment, great care should be taken to look for possible underlying causes. Frequently, one or more of the causes explored in this chapter can be identified.

WHY MOST CHILDREN MISBEHAVE

All normal children go through the same developmental stages, and most encounter similar kinds of out-of-school social and family conflicts. These factors contribute to ordinary—and often predictable—patterns of poor behavior in the classroom. A number of these "normal" behavior problems will be discussed here. Some extreme behavior problems and situations will be discussed at the end of the chapter.

Immaturity

So many problems between teachers and children are simply due to immaturity. Each month of a child's growth brings an improvement in motor coordination, spatial awareness, ability to

solve problems, ability to follow directions, and ability to inter-
act socially with others. Often children are placed in a certain
class, whether it be nursery school, kindergarten, or primary
school, only to discover that they are not quite as mature as most
of the other children in the class. The stress placed upon these
children can lead to misbehavior.

Some children who are immature for their age need an extra
three months to grow; some need another six months; some may
even need an entire year to catch up. This doesn't necessarily
mean that one child will always be less mature than others;
rather, the child's rate of growth, though normal in sequence, is
slower than that of others. An example is the child who is not
ready to learn to read until age seven, at which time he or she
suddenly becomes the best reader in the class. Such children
need to be protected from the daily trauma of being shamed and
pushed into attempting tasks that they are not developmentally
ready for. This pressure to learn produces unnecessary stress and
may cause emotional scars that will never be totally overcome.

Boredom

Boredom tends to be a catchall excuse for misbehavior. Usually,
however, there is more to it. Children with visual or auditory
problems often act bored because they are not taking in the
sensory information that other children are receiving. They seem
tuned out because they *are* tuned out. Children who are completely absorbed in their own thoughts may appear to be bored.
They may only be thinking how comfortable it is to be sitting
near the teacher or next to a special friend. Or they may be
thinking of more serious things. For example, a child might be
worried and depressed about a family crisis. A child so gripped
in an emotional vise won't be able to relate normally to classroom experiences.

Wrong class placement is another cause for children looking
as though they are bored. They may actually be bewildered
because they are too immature for their class group. On the
other hand, children who are too mature may feel that they don't
belong—and they don't. Such children may "turn themselves

off" and daydream about other, more satisfying, experiences. Daydreaming is very normal behavior for young children, and they shouldn't be faulted for it.

Continual academic failure will cause children to put on a facade of boredom, relating to the tenet that "it's better to be quiet and be thought dumb than to speak and remove all doubt." Gifted children sometimes need greater motivation than other children. They may be mentally brilliant or artistically talented, but they may have standards for themselves that are too high for them to meet. These children often need to be taught to undertake tasks for the joy of doing rather than for the purpose of achieving.

When a number of children in a particular classroom appear bored, the teacher needs to check his or her techniques and environment. Learning environments can be created that allow children to find many satisfying growth experiences on their own levels and with some degree of independence. Such environments decrease the need for children to rebel by antisocial or nonconformist behavior.

Curiosity

It is normal for children to want to increase their understanding of the environment through exploration, experimentation, questioning, and related activities. These kinds of experiences occur during normal play activities, reflecting children's intense desire to understand their environment. Rather than restricting their curiosity, thereby causing stress, the learning environment should promote and encourage it. When curiosity leads the children into difficulties, the teacher must remember that they are in a process of learning. When children are given legitimate opportunities to satisfy their curiosity, teachers will find that the need for behavioral control and correction is greatly reduced.

Visual and auditory disabilities

Very commonly, children in early childhood classrooms and kindergartens go for months with undetected auditory or visual problems. Such disabilities can cause great distress for children and, in turn, cause them to appear to misbehave. If you frequently feel that a particular child isn't listening, the child's hearing should be checked. And when you find that a child frequently bumps into things and drops things, that child's vision should be checked.

Very often these children come back with reports of 20/20 vision and normal hearing; yet the symptoms and resultant problems continue. Even though such children may physically hear and see well, they may be perceptually immature, not perceiving wholly what others see or hear. Frequently, this is merely a developmental problem, and the children only need more time to grow. However, some children are so deficient that they should be given remediation exercises to increase their perceptual acuity.

Much progress has been made in recent years toward defining the neurological relationship between perception and learning. Academic progress in the normal classroom is dependent on visual and auditory perception: Learning takes place in the brain; perception occurs in the brain; movement is directed by the brain. Children who have visual or auditory difficulties need a system of perceptual-motor training that will integrate the sensory modalities with other brain functions.

It has long been known that developmental exercises such as crawling, jumping, balancing, climbing, hopping, rolling, and spinning can enhance perceptual-motor skills. But new brain research and new findings in the area of the importance of the vestibular system in relation to perception and hemispheric integration are opening new doors to helping each child achieve maximum developmental potential. Families of children with serious perceptual problems should be referred to sources of appropriate remediation.

Family crises

It's important to find some means of communicating with parents on a regular basis so that you can remain alert to changing family conditions. It's especially important that the children's parents alert you to crises or significant changes at home or even in a parent's job. Occasionally, an insignificant matter may be the cause of negative behavior on the part of a child. Children sometimes misinterpret adult comments about comparatively minor issues and decide something horrible is going to happen. It is also possible for a child to be aware of a major crisis that the parents think is well hidden from the child.

When you realize there is a problem in a child's personal life, it may help to get the child to talk about it. Often, if you can find an opening — or can help the child find one — the child may get great relief simply from having an opportunity to express his or her concerns. Sometimes that is enough to balance the entire situation. On the other hand, if the child does not want to talk about it, you need to be understanding and hope that your extra care, attention, and patience will help lessen the child's inner turmoil.

Sensitivity to foods or environmental factors

In recent years, there has been much research into the extraordinary sensitivity that some people have to ordinary environmental factors. Symptoms may resemble those of common allergic reactions such as hay fever, or they may take the form of hyperactive behavior, in which case a vicious cycle can set in. The child's behavior is not accepted, and the child is subjected to repeated correction, criticism, confinement or other methods of control. Yet the child is physiologically unable to control the behavior, and punishment only aggravates the situation. The child builds up tremendous guilt and may become convinced of being a misfit. Misbehavior then becomes a reaction to others' expectations and finally to the child's own expectations, all of which are based on false assumptions.

Every effort should be made to find out why children act the way they do, especially in the case of hyperactivity. When environmental factors seem to be a cause, the following simple plan may be successful with many families:

1. Ask the parents to keep a daily diary of their child's activities. For each activity, time, place, and any unusual behavior should be listed. The parents should also make note of

anything unusual in the environment, such as fresh paint or other chemicals, animals, or unusual odors.

2. Have the parents keep a similar diary of everything the child ingests, both at mealtimes and between meals. The parents should note specific brand names of food (the ingredients listings of packaged foods may need to be examined in detail) and the time of each meal and snack. Half an hour after each meal and snack, they should note the child's behavior. An A to F rating scale can be used; A being the most acceptable behavior, F being the least desirable.

3. After two weeks, sit down with the parents to analyze the diaries for connections between environmental factors and behavior. You may want to have the parents continue the process for up to six weeks.

Family behavior

By the time they are toddlers, children have learned many variations in social and moral behavior by observing the behavior of their siblings and parents. Sometimes the behavior is negative. It may include crying easily, throwing temper tantrums, arguing, using retribution, and being hostile. Children may display habits they have learned at home, such as lying, not responding when spoken to, using vulgar language, or constantly complaining. Teachers have the double task of modeling acceptable behavior for such children and of finding ways to offset the unacceptable behavior the children see in their homes.

As teachers, we need to help and encourage children to learn new modes of behavior without punishing them for behaving the way their parents do. At the same time, we need to help their parents understand the process of modeling and the fact that it is usually one of the roots of antisocial and amoral behavior in small children.

Rhythm

Each of us is rhythmically unique. From birth on, some people naturally move slowly; some move fast. When children are forced into rhythms antithetical to their own natural paces, they are placed under a great deal of stress which frequently results in negative behavior. It is important that teachers watch carefully and get to know which of their students are early-in-the-day achievers and which do better when allowed time to get started. With a little care and concern, schedules can be manipulated to draw out the best each child has to offer.

Physical discomfort or illness

A child's physical condition has a direct relationship to school behavior. Hunger, fatigue, or the onset of illness can cause children to be short tempered or easily upset. When a normally well-behaved child demonstrates unusual behavior, check for headache, fever, earache, or stomachache. Children who appear listless or otherwise out of sorts should be allowed to rest. Red or watery eyes (with or without a runny nose) should be cause for concern. Even if such symptoms are due to an allergy rather than a pending cold or flu, they make the child feel uncomfortable and thus may cause a change in behavior. Check, too, for tight clothes or something poking or chafing the child.

Chronic, subtle illnesses may cause cooperative children to develop negative patterns of behavior. It is important that teachers, who can sometimes be more objective, alert parents to such changes in children's actions.

Reinforcement

Adults often unwittingly reinforce misbehavior by overreacting to it. By overreacting, I mean expressing extreme emotional reactions—shouting, threatening, coercing, nagging, or using spanking or other physical punishment. It has been shown time and again that children who are frequently punished for negative behavior require more and more frequent punishment. They become conditioned to the idea that misbehavior is expected of them and that it gets attention. Angry, confused, or lonely children will repeat offenses in order to control or get attention from the adults in their world. If it works, they will repeat it over and over again. Recognizing a pattern of reinforcement can be the first step toward instituting discipline that will help such children learn positive behavior patterns without reinforcing the negative ones.

Too many *nos*

How many times do you say *no* or *don't* or *not now* during the course of a school day? Children do need to be given firm limits. They do need to be told when what they are doing or planning is inappropriate in regard to social mores, safety, or respect of property. But too many *nos* will negate our best intentions and make children feel harangued and inhibited.

The process of growth and development takes many years and is best accomplished through trial and error under the gentle guidance of adults. Our role as teachers is to help children develop the skills to make appropriate decisions. We not only need to give them many opportunities to experience the consequences of their own actions, but we must also protect them and others by giving clear, explicit reasons for the *nos* that we give them. Many abrupt *nos* can be avoided by the use of more considerate alternatives that take the children's feelings, your feelings, and the traditional power struggle into account. Here are some examples:

HASTY RESPONSE	CONSIDERED RESPONSE
No, you can't paint without an apron.	*I know you feel uncomfortable in an apron, but when you paint, you need to wear one to keep your clothes from getting any paint on them.*
No, you can't play soccer today.	*I know you would like to play soccer, but after that bad nosebleed you had, it would be better for you to do something that is less active.*

No, you can't have that book. Larry is reading it.	*That book has good horse stories in it. When Larry is through with it, you may have it.*
No, you can't have two helpings.	*I'm glad you enjoyed the fruit salad. There's not enough for seconds today, but next time we'll make more.*
Don't touch that.	*I'm glad you noticed my new plant. Plants are for looking at. Touching the leaves can hurt them.*
No, you absolutely can't do that. It's too dangerous.	*That looks pretty high to me. I will stand close and watch while you try it out. But if it feels too high up, you let me know and I'll help you to get down.*
No, that's not what the recipe says.	*That might make the recipe taste different, but it would be interesting to try. Why don't you put just a little in this separate cup and see whether it's a good idea or not.*
No, that's against our rules.	*We have a rule about that. Maybe we can change the rule. Let's see how sharp that knife is. It seems too sharp to me. I think you need to wait until I have time to help you use it.*

It is important for children to learn that the difference between *no* and *yes* is a matter of careful consideration, not a hasty response. If they observe you carefully weighing the pros and cons of a situation, they will learn to do so too.

Manipulative or masked behavior

Among the most difficult situations to handle are those in which children mask a feeling or need — usually by behaving inappropriately. Children don't usually know they are "coding" their behavior; they are simply using a defense mechanism they have developed in response to basic insecurities in their relationships with others. For example, take a child who has broken some object and provokes punishment by starting a fight with another child rather than by admitting the accident. Such a child may be feeling anxiety and guilt, which are too difficult for the child to cope with. Hitting another child may be easier to handle. Another example is a child who is domineering to the point of alienating other children. Such a child really wants friends, but, because of a very poor self-image, needs to be in control of all situations. Such a child lacks trust and needs much help in working out hidden insecurities.

Punishment is not what these children need. They need to have people listen to them and give them feedback. They need to have their self-confidence built up, one small step at a time, until they can cope with flexibility. They need to experience honesty and kept promises in order to kindle or rekindle their own feelings of trust. They also need opportunity for dramatic play. Through dramatic play, these children may, in time, work out their misperceptions of the world about them. With support from caring adults, they may eventually be able to overcome their need to use manipulative behavior.

Testing limits

Very often the only reason why a child misbehaves is that the child is going through a developmental stage in which testing limits is very important. A constant theme in childhood is the need children have to feel in control of their lives as much as possible. Testing limits is one of the ways they try out that control. On the one hand, they get an idea and start to try it out, watching you to see whether you will approve and how far they can go if you disapprove. This helps them to build their feelings of autonomy. On the other hand, an insecure child may deliberately try to do something he or she knows you disapprove of to test whether you really care. Children are comforted to know that an adult will help them control their actions and their emotions.

Personality conflicts

Personality conflicts are not something that many teachers will admit to openly. Nonetheless, there are, unfortunately, some children whose personalities clash with their teacher's. It isn't very mysterious that teachers, confronted with classrooms of total strangers, will occasionally find some children they can't relate to. Perhaps a child's demeanor or facial expression is reminiscent of someone the teacher dislikes. Perhaps it is the child's voice, movements, or some more subtle form of communication that annoys the teacher.

The ideal situation would be to be able to say to a supervisor, "Please place this child in another class. It's very important to me." But such situations are rare. Therefore, it is our responsibility to expose ourselves to close contact with such a child little by little until we break through irrational barriers. In the meantime, extra care must be taken not to make this child the scapegoat when things go wrong. Often it is our very rejection, even when unspoken, that will cause poor behavior patterns in children.

EXTREME CASES

As you read this book, you may say to yourself, "That may be OK for most children, but she doesn't know Diane," or "I'd like to see her try to work some of those tricks with Manuel," or "Well, she doesn't know my kids." Perhaps you may think, "She must have all nicely behaved children or children with no problems" or even "She made it all up. She's living in a dream world. She should meet some *real* kids."

This book is about real kids. I have worked for many years with normal children who bite, kick, push, fight, yell, swear, break things, throw things, knock things down, talk back, insult others, lie, steal, tease, taunt, and do all of the other things that children are subject to doing and that gets them into trouble with adults and even with other children.

In addition, over the many years of my experience as a school director, I have frequently enrolled rejects from other schools. I have sometimes taken children who had been dismissed from as many as two or three schools over a three-month period. I've been so badly bitten by a two-year-old that I needed medical attention, and I've been called unprintable names by a four-year-old. I've had money stolen from my purse by a six-year-old and had my face slapped by an eight-year-old. I've gotten very angry and frustrated and full of despair, just as you have many times. I've been discouraged, embarrassed, and made to feel like a fool. But I've never knowingly rejected a child and I've never deliberately punished a child. I've spent hour upon hour alone with children, helping them to sort out their feelings and studying them to find causes for their lack of behavioral control.

Working with hostile children

Realizing that uncooperative children and hostile, belligerent children may have lacked appropriate professional guidance, I try to compensate for that lack in the everyday course of my relationship with such children. They have usually known much coercion, threats, reprisals, punishments, and impatience. They have been berated and confused. The treatment they have received modeled ways to coerce, threaten, punish, and berate others. These children develop such a poor self-image that they can only function in ways that help them live up to that image. They are literally starved for affection; they don't let anyone get close to them because they don't feel close to anyone. They are lonely and full of despair. They feel so hated that they spend much of their time retaliating with hate towards others. In most cases their uncooperativeness will have been reinforced by the very discipline imposed on them for that behavior.

My challenge is to introduce these children into a world of acceptance — a world in which it is only their behavior, not themselves, that is rejected. Everyone who is involved with such children needs to express new expectations for the children and practice new ways of interrelating positively. Problem solving to change the behavior of belligerent children requires careful planning, cooperation, persistence, and patience. (See pages 167–173 for a description of systematic problem solving.) Does it work? In the majority of cases, yes. In approaching each child's needs, three steps should be taken: (1) search out the cause of the behavior, (2) develop a consistent plan for helping the child learn new modes of behavior, and (3) recognize your need to make changes in the way you react to the child. Once the cause of a behavior is found, it needs to be remedied; once the cause is remedied, the job is still not done.

One day I was sitting in my office at a conference table, accepting a check from a woman who had just enrolled her daughter in our school. We were sitting next to each other, and as she wrote, I could feel the movement of her arm as it brushed against mine. Suddenly, a teacher came stomping into the office holding a crying, arm-flailing, screaming child. "I just can't have you in my room right now," the teacher said as he plunked the child in the chair next to mine.

The moving arm next to me froze. I, too, momentarily froze. Then I reached for some paper and crayons, looked at the child, Tekatcha, and said, "Your teacher was sure mad, wasn't he?" Tekatcha nodded her head, her screams slowing down to quiet sobs. "And you look like you're very mad, too." Again she nodded her head, this time quite vigorously. I gave her a large piece of white paper and some crayons and said, "Why don't you draw on this paper how mad you are? Then I'll know how you feel." Still sobbing, she scribbled vigorously with the black crayon I had handed her, back and forth, back and forth. Gradually her movements slowed. She reached for a pink crayon and began making little circular shapes—then a blue, a green, a yellow. Her sobs gave way to a humming sound.

The frozen arm next to mine relaxed. "How beautiful," the woman said, as she finished writing her check. Later on I explained to her that four months earlier, Tekatcha had been crossing a street with her parents when an automobile struck down her father. She had seen her father lying there, dead. The mother had gone into shock and was still suffering tremendous fear and depression. The child had begun screaming at the time. Periodically—several times a day—she relived the horrible experience. She had been rejected by several child care agencies. I had agreed to take her for a two-week period while her mother was being resettled. I had also told her teacher that the child should be brought into the office whenever she started screaming and that I would deal with it.

Tekatcha's case, of course, was an extreme one; though a therapeutic environment and treatment were urgent, we could only provide an accepting environment as a stopgap. But her case demonstrates that even with extreme cases, a humane, nonpunitive approach can work. It can work with hostile, belligerent children. It can work with sarcastic, sassy, arrogant children. It will work with children who are noisy and overactive and with children who are sullen and morose. It may take a great deal of trial and error before you find the methods that work best with particular children. In general, there are four steps you must take when you begin working with such children:

1. Give them an accepting, consistent, caring environment. Most of the children who have trouble in the classroom are having similar problems in their homes. In addition to enduring the normal tensions of family living, they are often faced with ongoing inconsistencies and rejection when communicating with their parents. They feel unloved and unwanted. Compare the patterns of communication illustrated in the following examples. The children from these households would arrive at school in very different moods.

BELLIGERENT PATTERN OF INTERACTION	COOPERATIVE PATTERN OF INTERACTION
Good morning, darling, time to get up. Time to get up, I said. If you don't get up I'll come in there and do it for you. Damn it. I said get up right now.	*Good morning, darling. Time to get up and get dressed. Here are the clothes we got ready last night. Call me if you need help. We can eat breakfast as soon as you've brushed your teeth.*
Did you brush your teeth? Are you sure you're telling me the truth?	*I'm glad I have this chance to sit and eat breakfast with you because I won't see you again until dinnertime. To-night after dinner we can read that new rocket book.*
Not that shirt. It's filthy. If you had put it in the hamper like I told you to it wouldn't be lying around for you to put on. No! Don't you have any brains? Not that shirt! It's cold out today. Don't argue with me. Wear this warm shirt. Boy, you sure know how to get someone in a bad mood in the morning. All you think about is yourself.	

When you greet the children at school, think in terms of the kind of morning they might already have had. Look for signals in their body language — their movements and postures, their tension (or lack of it), their rhythms, the tones of their voices, and similar clues. Let them know that you are glad they have come to school. Tell them something about what's going to happen during the day, and that you're looking forward to interesting things to do and talk about together. (Each day *should* be special. Every moment, every hour in a child's life experiences is important. Children don't need to be around adults who think, "I hope I can get through this day," but rather, "I wonder how I can help him or her have a good day.")

2. Use the "magic list" of disciplinary methods in Part 2. The list suggests alternatives to punitive discipline; it is like magic, and it will work. Choose the alternatives that are most appropriate for you and the child. Be patient, remembering always that as a teacher, your job is to promote growth and learning. You need to communicate in such ways that these children can learn more socially acceptable ways of responding and interacting. You need to help build their self-esteem and help them experience acceptance.

3. Get to know the children's parents. It is important for you to establish lines of communication with the parents of all your children, but it is especially urgent that you do so with the parents of those who have difficulty cooperating or controlling their actions. Working together, you can trace the causes for the poor behavior. You may also be able to involve them in a systematic approach to changing the child's behavior. Make every effort to interest them in attending parent education groups where, by discussing problems and sharing ideas with other parents, they can learn methods of intervention and of coping.

4. Begin problem solving. With or without the parents' help, initiate a program of systematic problem solving (see pages 167–173). As previously stated, every inappropriate behavior has a cause, just as every appropriate behavior has a cause. Everything we do, we do because we want something. We have to find out what children's *real* wants are and then find ways of supplying those wants if they are appropriate or changing them if they are inappropriate.

Working with clinically disturbed children

Disturbed children require more care and consideration when they misbehave than do normal children. Often this misbehavior takes very active, destructive forms. Nonetheless, it is essential that you convey to these children, by your own actions, that you are going to help them find ways of behaving that will not elicit constant rejection by others. These children need to know that you think they are wonderful people and that you want to change not them, but only some of their ways of acting. A great deal of patience and cooperation are required of all who are involved. Unless yours is a program for disturbed children, you must evaluate carefully each child that you undertake to help. Mainstreaming has many advantages, but you must recognize your own limitations. Mainstream only the number of children that can be handled by the staff you have, the school philosophy under which you operate, and the needs and problems of the other children who are enrolled. Knowing your own limitations, being ready to seek professional assistance and guidance when you need them, and being ready to admit failure when you are unable to reach a particular child are all important considerations in mainstreaming children.

Emergencies

There are emergency situations in which drastic action must be taken because of extremely irrational or violent behavior on the part of a child. Emergencies are not part of the teaching-learning process. They are not punishment. They are simply emergencies.

When someone's health or safety is at risk, you must take immediate action. Do whatever is necessary to avert disaster. For example, if three-year-old Tommy is ready to clobber Janie (same age) on the back of the head with a ten-inch metal truck, grab the truck out of Tommy's hands. If you're too far away, shout "Tommy!" long enough to distract him. Then say, "Put that truck down right now!" very firmly and positively, leaving no doubt in Tommy's mind that he must really put it down. Simultaneously, you should be moving toward him to physically enforce your order if Tommy doesn't respond. Meanwhile, you will have interrupted his action long enough to keep him from hurting Janie.

There are occasions when children become so angry that they decide to run away from school. There should always be an adult in attendance who can run faster and can manage to get ahead of a child. When children see that no one is coming after them, they will usually turn around and return of their own accord. However, you are responsible for each child's safety. So even though ignoring a would-be runaway may be the best course to take, you may not dare to do so because common sense tells you the child really might be in danger.

From time to time I have worked with children who have been rejected by other programs, who face nothing but rejection in their personal lives, and whom I have allowed to come to school in the hopes that our accepting environment would help them to gain self-esteem. There are times when these children become so emotionally overwrought that one needs to take drastic action to help them regain control of themselves. The following are some methods I have used with out-of-control children:

1. Put your arms around the child from the rear and hug tight until he or she calms down.

2. Remove a large, screaming, arm-flailing child from an area of disturbance by picking the child up around the waist. Hold the child at a forty-five degree angle, head down, with the legs reaching over one of your shoulders. You can carry a child in this position without being hit or kicked and thus remove the child from an "audience" without a fight. The lifting and carrying should be done firmly but gently; there should be no hint of punishment in it.

   I have seldom used this carrying method on any child more than once. No matter how out of control the behavior seems to be, if I reach for the waist as I have done before, the child usually says, "I'll come by myself." Merely by saying this, the child regains control over seemingly uncontrollable actions.

3. Belligerent, withdrawn, or hyperactive children often avoid looking you in the eyes. There have been times when I have been able to regain such a child's attention by having someone else hold the child's head gently but firmly so that it can't be moved from side to side. I, at the same time, will hold the child gently by the arms and look directly into his or her eyes, saying, "It's all right. I know you're very angry. You can tell me all about it. First I need you to sit down right here so I know where you are," or something appropriate to

the situation. Talking to the child while looking directly into the eyes usually establishes a communication that enables me to use a restorative approach such as discussion, helping the child to express feelings in a legitimate manner, humor, or whatever I feel will help meet the child's immediate needs — and mine.

Everyone responds somewhat differently to imminent danger. Teachers or other responsible adults should not fear reprisal if their actions conflict with the school's philosophy or usual practice. It is important that they be constantly alert to what children are doing, anticipate potential dangers, and, when health and safety are threatened, know that they have the freedom to take whatever action they feel is necessary to cope with the emergency.

Part II
THE MAGIC LIST: ALTERNATIVES TO PUNITIVE DISCIPLINE

THE MAGIC LIST:
ALTERNATIVES TO PUNITIVE DISCIPLINE

Anticipate trouble
Give gentle reminders
Distract to a positive model
Inject humor
Offer choices
Give praise or compliments
Offer encouragement
Clarify messages
Overlook small annoyances
Deliberately ignore provocations
Reconsider the situation
Point out natural,
or logical, consequences
Provide renewal time
Give hugs and caring
Arrange discussion
among the children
Provide discussion with an adult

Disciplinary Attitudes: An Introduction to Nondiscipline Discipline

5 Children and adults can waste a great deal of energy engaging in conflict under the guise of discipline. Indeed, traditional methods of discipline too often fail us because they are not very effective. Children need guidance — that is an accepted fact. They need help developing skills to make wise decisions for themselves. They need protection for their health and safety. They need limits, directions, and rules to abide by, but the discipline directed toward them must be geared to the development of self-respect, healthy interpersonal relationships, and skills in problem solving. We must look to alternative methods that will be effective as well as lessen pointless conflict. This requires a change in our basic attitudes about discipline. My program of Nondiscipline Discipline, which offers alternatives to punitive, abusive, and irrational control of children, exemplifies such a change.

TRADITIONAL DISCIPLINARY ATTITUDES

Unfortunately, many of our child-rearing and educational traditions are based on negative attitudes. The adult's responsibility has been to prevent children from doing wrong rather than to pursue the more joyful task of helping children to do right. Such a negative approach has fostered negative control techniques: threats, disapproval, and punishment to create guilt, fear, and submission. For years it was taken for granted that just because a child "belonged" to a parent, that parent had the right to physically abuse the child. We don't say "abuse," however; we say "spank." When methods that involve force and verbal and physical abuse are used, children suffer shame and humiliation.

The following are categories and examples of punishment common in classrooms today. As you read them, think of whether you have used any of them. Consider whether they have contributed to harmony and cooperation between you and the children and try to identify the underlying attitudes they express.

- Childish control: "You're a bad boy." "No, no, no." "If you bite anyone again, I'll bite *you*."
- Punitive control: "Just for that, no recesses for you all week." "You can spend the rest of the day in the office." "Write 'I will follow directions' one hundred times."
- Abusive verbal control: "Why can't you hurry up? What a slowpoke! I've told you twenty times how to hurry up, hurry up, hurry up!" "What's wrong? Are you too stupid to figure out how to do it?" "Now everyone is going to have a shortened lunch period—all because of you."
- Abusive physical control: This includes spanking; biting back; slapping; pinching; gripping the shoulder, neck, arm, face, or other part of the body tightly; pulling the child by the hair or ear; pushing the child; knocking the child down; rapping the knuckles; poking; or the like.
- Irrational control: This includes any combinations of the other types of control accompanied or characterized by intense anger, harangues, fierce expressions, threatening gestures, and the like.

In the long run, harsh discipline usually doesn't work. Children who are spanked, for example, are spanked over and over again. What we are really teaching them by such punitive methods is that violence, abuse, and humiliation of others is acceptable. Teachers, too, suffer shame and humiliation when they find themselves shouting at children and punishing them over and over again. Professional and personal self-esteem suffer. Everyone loses when time is wasted in patrolling and punishing students.

NONDISCIPLINE DISCIPLINE ATTITUDES

As long as our system of discipline is based on the expectation that children will misbehave, children will live up to that expectation; if we use discipline based on the attitude that children want to cooperate, children will live up to that expectation instead. Nondiscipline Discipline is based on friendly, caring attitudes toward the health, development, and needs of children. It gives careful regard to feelings and emotions, to unique differences between individuals, and to preserving an atmosphere of acceptance, tolerance, and patience.

Nondiscipline Discipline permits you to be a teacher, not a mock dictator or prison guard. This is a rational, analytical approach. It asks you to ask yourself, in each instance of a child's misbehavior, "How can I help this child find an alternative way of behaving without reinforcing the behavior I would like to see changed?" The assumption — the attitude — underlying this kind of discipline is that it will help children learn and grow in harmony with one another. There is also an assumption that if you want children to change, you must be willing to change as well.

Setting clear rules and precise limits

A wholesome learning environment which practices Nondiscipline Discipline is one in which you, the teacher, with the cooperation and knowledge of the children, have set explicit, understandable limits and rules for personal and group conduct. As you set out your basic guidelines, you may find that the following considerations will enhance the process.

• Bring the children into the process of setting limits and rules. They will adhere more closely to rules they have helped to establish and evaluate than ones which have been imposed on them arbitrarily. Including children in such processes helps them learn responsibility and discriminative thinking.

• Be honest. Tell the children what behavior really bothers you, even if it is only an idiosyncrasy of yours and not an actual infraction of rules.

• Be realistic. Most rules are logically founded in concerns for health, safety, and care of property. The ability to use logic doesn't begin to develop until the elementary school years, and even then it takes time for children to become skilled in its use. Explanations of cause and effect must take into account the more immature perceptions of preschool-age children.

• Be democratic. Rules must be fair. They must apply equally to all. They must be geared to the ages and developmental capabilities of the children.

Soliciting cooperation

Once you have committed yourself to nondisciplinary attitudes, established clear rules and precise limits, and begun utilizing good communication methods (see pages 111–116), you can begin to adapt the following principles for ensuring children's cooperation with your positive efforts.

• Be precise. When you make a request, make it clear to whom you are addressing your comments. Politely and firmly say what you want and when you want it. Assume that they would rather cooperate than not.

• Be consistent. Make sure your requests are in keeping with established rules and practices.

• Be fair. Be sure the requests you make apply equally to everyone.

• Avoid repetition. If you fail to get someone's attention, you might say, "I called you," or "Joan, I'm waiting for you." This will usually elicit the attention of a child who heard you but didn't listen.

• Enforce your requests. You need to be assertive but at the same time remain kind, caring, and gentle. Following through with a request can mean guiding a child to some location by cupping your hand under the child's elbow or gently taking the child's hand. In an emergency, you may need to lift up a child bodily.

• Don't argue. Be persistent but don't provoke a confrontation. If you're unable to remove the child bodily or to enforce what you have requested without an argument, it may be wise to walk away from it.

• Remain flexible. Sometimes you might say, "I can see you won't cooperate today. I'll ask you another day."

THE MAGIC LIST OF ALTERNATIVES

Because traditional methods of discipline are so ingrained that they are almost automatic responses, I have developed a "magic list" of alternatives to them. Each item on the list is described in detail in Part II. Most teachers have used these methods at one time or another, and many may have items to add to the magic list.

TRADITIONAL PUNITIVE RESPONSE	THE MAGIC LIST OF ALTERNATIVES
React impulsively	Anticipate trouble
Issue sarcasm and threats	Give gentle reminders
Find fault and scold	Distract to a positive model
Be grouchy and irritable	Inject humor
Make rigid demands	Offer choices
Belittle or ignore	Give praise or compliments
Criticise and coerce	Offer encouragement
Make ambiguous comments	Clarify messages
Nit-pick or nag	
	Overlook small annoyances
React hastily and automatically	Deliberately ignore provocations
Be stubborn and unbending	Reconsider the situation
Punish	
	Point out natural, or logical, consequences

Impose isolation
Make authoritarian
demands
Humiliate, impose guilt,
and punish
Lecture

Provide renewal time
Give hugs and caring

Arrange discussion among
the children
Provide discussion with an
adult

Which alternative to choose?

There is no simple answer as to which alternative to choose.

Usually, any one of several alternatives can be selected for a particular incident. The important thing to remember is that *automatic* responses are self-defeating. Each child, being an individual with unique characteristics, personality, and skills, deserves individual consideration. Each situation is likewise unique and must be evaluated as to the degree and method of intervention that will produce the desired results.

In the following example, several alternative responses are given:

Allison, age nine, and Jennie, age eight, were quarreling over the use of the dictionary, disturbing the others in the classroom.

TYPICAL RESPONSE

Teacher: *You two girls come here. You should know better than that. I'm ashamed of you. Now, tell me what that quarreling was all about.*
Allison: *Well, I needed to look up a word and . . .*
Jennie (simultaneously): *She grabbed the dictionary!*
Teacher: *I think you're both to blame. I want you to fin-ish your assignment and then come to the desk. I'll give you both an extra*

ALTERNATIVE RESPONSE

GIVE GENTLE
REMINDERS — USE GERUNDS
Teacher: *Girls, sharing.*
(They immediately stop quarreling and take turns.)
or
Teacher: *It needs to be quiet in here so people can study.*
(Again, they immediately stop quarreling and take turns.)

RECONSIDER THE SITUATION
Teacher: *One of you can use my dictionary. We should*

assignment to do during
your lunch period. That
should teach you how to behave. (The teacher has
taken a very minor inci-
dent and blown it up out of
proportion. Instead of
helping the girls toward a
different kind of behavior,
she only serves to humiliate them, lower their self-
esteem, inflict guilt, and
increase their inner stress.)

have two here, anyway.
(The girls look apprecia-
tively at the teacher.)
Girls: (simultaneously):
Thank you.
or
Teacher: *I'm sorry we have
only one dictionary. It makes
it hard, but you know how to
take turns using it. We'll try
to order another one to have
soon.*

ARRANGE DISCUSSION AMONG
THE CHILDREN
Teacher: *I don't know what
the problem is, but I think
you two should discuss it
with each other quietly.*
(Teacher goes back to her
desk. The girls talk quietly
for a moment or two and
then appear to be happily
sharing the dictionary.)

OFFER CHOICES
Teacher: *You'll have to decide whether you want to
share the dictionary, go to
Miss Karen's room and borrow hers, or just not use a
dictionary at all. Which do
you choose?*
Jennie: *Let's share.*
Allison: OK.

OVERLOOK SMALL ANNOYANCES;
GIVE GENTLE REMINDERS
Teacher (to the class): *Let's
keep things quiet so you can
finish your work before
lunch.* (In addressing the
entire class, the teacher

gives the girls a gentle reminder without making an
issue of their quarreling.)

Any one of the alternatives is a satisfactory response, since they each serve the purpose of helping the girls find a way of solving their difficulties.

Of course, you won't use all the alternatives from the magic list at once. You'll learn to use them gradually when they seem comfortable and appropriate. To help you get started using Nondiscipline Discipline in your classroom, follow these steps:

1. Read all of the alternatives from beginning to end. Put a paper clip on those pages you wish to reread for clarification or to check their validity.
2. Try out one alternative each day. If you can enlist the aid of co-workers, all the better.
3. Evaluate each of the alternatives as to how well it suits your teaching style and personality, how comfortable you are with it, and how well it works with the children.
4. Post the magic list at two or three places in the classroom. Refer to it quickly when you're in doubt about how to respond to a given situation. Except in an emergency, take the time to decide which alternative will be most effective.
5. Modify the magic list by adding your own ideas.
6. With children who have significant or chronic behavior problems, use the utmost patience while you look for prob-able causes and devise appropriate solutions to those prob-lems. (See pages 167–173.)

I post the magic list and use it daily as a reminder of alternatives I can choose from. It helps me in the ongoing development and refinement of my own nondisciplinary attitudes. Consciously choosing from the magic list of alternatives instead of resorting to the more typical, traditional reactions has opened many new doors for me — doors to the joys of teaching and the wonders of childhood. Using this or a similar list can do the same for you.

Alternatives: Preventing Inappropriate Behavior

6 Prevention is often the best cure. This concept applies to behavior problems in the classroom as well as to health and maintenance problems in the world at large. The five alternatives discussed in this chapter are particularly useful in nipping trouble in the bud.

ANTICIPATE TROUBLE

Anticipating trouble is one of the most important alternatives; with it you can prevent trouble before it starts. Anticipating means knowing the ages and personalities of your students and being able to guess at their likely responses to various situations. Through anticipation, you can arrange materials and activities for children to use as soon as they arrive at school, thus motivating productive behavior. You can, in general, control the physical environment so as to minimize stress and promote trust and cooperation.

Anticipating also means being alert to the emotional environment. Sometimes the human elements of the environment are obvious, as in the case of children who elicit such comments as "Every time those two sit next to each other, they get into a fight." The anticipating teacher would make sure that those children did not sit next to each other.

Sometimes the emotional variables are more subtle and, therefore, less predictable. By carefully observing your students' interactions with one another, you will be able to tell by their body language and verbal communication when a situation is beginning to deteriorate. If they cannot solve the difficulty by themselves, your prompt intervention *before* trouble begins can prevent a serious confrontation.

The following are some examples of how anticipating trouble works:

TYPICAL RESPONSE	ANTICIPATING TROUBLE
You two boys stop that fighting right now. Every time you get next to each other you end up fighting. You heard me. Here! Tom, come and sit over here. I can't trust you two to be together. (The feelings generated are embarrassment, belligerence, tension, and lowered self-esteem.)	*Tom, you look rather comfortable over there, but for right now I'd like you to come and sit over here next to Susan.* (A tense situation is avoided politely and no negative feelings are generated.)
You get back here. You can't leave that stuff in such a big mess. Get that cleaned up right now. You should know that without my even telling you. (The same feelings are generated.)	*We're going to get ready for lunch in a little while. As soon as you finish that row, you can start putting those things away. If you like, you can play with them again tomorrow.* (Caring and understanding are expressed, helpfulness is encouraged, and happy anticipation for the next day is set.)
Now see what you've done. You know you can't play ball next to those big windows. That's going to cost a lot of money to repair. (A window	*The window might break if the ball hits it. That would be dangerous. You children may go over to that area to to play. I'll be there in a few*

is broken, and children are made to feel fearful and guilty.)	minutes. *I'd like to watch the game.* (The teacher models appropriate caution, caring, and interest while averting trouble.)

It was three days before the winter recess and the holiday season. The children throughout the school were very keyed up, as were their parents and teachers. The staff discussed among themselves the importance of anticipating more irrational behavior on the part of the children than usual. They made plans for several steps that could be taken in anticipation of the heightened excitement and tensions.

TYPICAL RESPONSE	ANTICIPATING TROUBLE
Hurry up now. Everybody has to get to work. You'll never get these gifts done on time if you stand around talking. Here, who's working on this? Come on, come on. Don't waste so much time. Oh, my goodness. We have so much to do. I don't know how we'll ever get through the next three days. (The teacher is so keyed up that both her classroom planning and her own demeanor is adding to the already heightened tension of the children. The day will probably end up with several emotional confrontations between the children and between the children and the teacher.)	*Here are several new puzzles and games that I've been saving for you. You can check them out for about half an hour. Then we'll go for a neighborhood walk, and later you can help me make a big smile collage for the whole school.* (Two weeks earlier, the teacher had sent home carefully mounted artwork that the children had done themselves. An accompanying note to the parents read, "Please help your child use this artwork in whatever gift-giving customs your family practices." The teacher has planned an interesting, low-key morning in anticipation of the children's heightened tensions. The walk helps use up surplus energy in a noncompetitive way.)

It had been indoor weather for five weeks. Today was the first day that the skies were clear and the children could go outdoors to play. However, five weeks of being indoors in very gloomy weather had put a lot of pressure on everyone, and both the children and the adults were very irritable.

TYPICAL RESPONSE	ANTICIPATING TROUBLE
Well, it's really a nice day for a change. It would be nice to go out and play, but you've behaved so badly, I think we'll just stay in until you learn the rules again. (Rather than helping these children regain their self-control, the teacher punishes them, possibly upsetting them to the point that their behavior will deteriorate even more.)	*We're lucky that the weather has finally cleared up enough so we can go outdoors to play. First, let's go over some of our rules so we can really enjoy the nice day and have an especially good time playing together.* (Anticipating that the children might be overenthusiastic in their play after being indoors for so long, the teacher takes the time to review the school rules and limits with the children, thereby helping everyone enjoy their playtime more.)

Stevie, almost four years old, arrived at school in an unusually heightened emotional state. His family was preparing to move and the moving truck was to come the next day. Everything at home was in a turmoil.

TYPICAL RESPONSE	ANTICIPATING TROUBLE
Teacher: *OK, Stevie, calm down now. I can see what kind of day we're going to have with you. Now you'll just have to straighten yourself out. You know, you're not the only one who's ever moved. People do it every day, and there's nothing wrong with it.* (Within five	**Teacher:** *Stevie, you're really excited about moving, aren't you? Here, let me rock you for a while and you can tell me about it.* **Stevie** (crying): *Where's Mamma?* **Teacher:** *Your mamma went home to get everything ready for the truck.*

minutes Stevie has knocked one child out of her chair, and bitten another.)
Teacher: *I knew it. I want you to just sit at this table over here by yourself for the rest of the morning. That will straighten you out.*

Stevie: *Are Mamma and Daddy going in the truck?*
Teacher: *No, Stevie. The truck man will come to your house tomorrow. You'll stay home tomorrow and see the truck come. Then Mamma and Daddy will go in your car with you. They can't go with the truck man.*
Stevie: *Can I go play?* (Anticipating his worries, this teacher puts Stevie at ease by helping him to express himself and by clarifying things for him before his emotions cause him to lose control of his behavior.)

GIVE GENTLE REMINDERS

Gentle reminders are never sarcastic. Comments that are demeaning or embarrassing have no place in the development of wholesome interpersonal relationships. When they are properly conveyed, however, gentle reminders can fulfill for children the need to have someone on whom they can depend and to whom they can look for helping in maintaining their self-control.

Using gerunds

Gerunds can be used as gentle reminders and are especially effective with preschool children. They also work well in pressure situations with older children. I discovered the usefulness of gerunds as reminders quite accidentally. At one time in my career, I worked for a European-born psychologist. She frequently used gerunds in working with children. She not only had an innate ability to understand children and to create harmonious environments and curricula for them, but she never had to say anything to them twice. Later, I found myself frequently using her manner of talking to children. The children responded much more consistently when I used that method than when I spoke to them normally.

When I analyzed this curious phenomenon, I realized that if I say to a child, "We don't run in the halls," the child can respond with, "You don't run in the halls, but I do." If I say, "Don't run in the halls," the child can respond with, "OK. Later I won't run in the halls, even though I am doing it now." But if I say, "Walking," the child will slow down immediately. The gerund has the same connotation as the command, "Stop running right now." Gerunds give you a method of seeking responses from children by use of the shortest, simplest, gentlest type of reminder. You can use them in virtually every situation.

TYPICAL RESPONSE	USING GERUNDS AS REMINDERS
Please sit down and wait.	Waiting.
Everyone is supposed to be helping to pick up the blocks.	John, Susan, helping.
Please sit still while I go get a storybook to read to you.	Sitting quietly everyone.
Jennie, please don't bother Armando. He doesn't like that.	Leaving Armando alone, please.
Watch out how you're carrying that. It's spilling.	Not spilling, please.
Keep your fingers out of those cupcakes. That's going to be for our party.	Not touching.
Don't just let it lie there on the floor. Pick it up.	Picking it up.
This is a quiet time. Everyone is supposed to be resting. Be quiet now, everyone.	Resting.
Please be quiet and listen.	Listening.

When I asked you children to   Cleaning up.
clean up this room, I meant
for you to do it right now.

The advantage of these and similar short phrases is that children seem to interpret them as really meaning "right now." The children respond to them easily; I think they appreciate the lack of lengthy tirades.

My very favorite gerund reminder is "playing nicely." Whenever I see cooperative behavior beginning to deteriorate, I approach the children and say, casually but definitely, "Playing nicely." It says to children, "I know you are capable of playing nicely and remembering the rules. I'll just give you a little reminder that will make the remembering easier for you." It is very effective with two-, three-, four-, and even five-year-olds. Time and again I have seen children stop what they were doing, think for a moment, and then resume their activity with less belligerence or moodiness.

The effectiveness of gerunds is evident when you hear children use them with one another — especially when you see a little four-year-old looking at a group of peers and saying, "Playing nicely." Parents have reported that their children, when being nagged or lectured without having been given a chance to explain, will occasionally say, "Mother, listening" or "Waiting, please."

Some people have expressed concern that the use of gerunds as gentle reminders will result in children growing up using incorrect language. In response, I can only say that I have seen hundreds of children go though this system to become excellent academic students. The use of gerunds as gentle reminders does not carry over into children's regular use of language; just as their teachers do, however, the children may call forth a phrase or two that suits their purposes when they need instant response.

The technique is especially useful with older children who have been consistently hard to handle. Children who are seven, eight, or nine years old and have frequent problems of misbehavior may be surprised into cooperation by the use of gerund reminders as a new approach:

- To the child who is poised to run from the room before the bell has rung: "Waiting."
- To the child who walks up to another child with clenched fists, ready to start a fight: "Touching softly."
- To two children who have been quarreling and who are letting their emotions get out of control: "Discussing."
- To the child who is glancing at a neighbor's paper during a test: "Keeping your eyes on your own paper."
- To the child whose excitement is causing him to start off a string of crude remarks to another: "Talking nicely."

And to the teacher reading this book: "Trying it."

Reminding older children

Third graders and some older children respond well to reminders such as "Oh, oh! Remembering!" or "I'm watching you," or even just their names. As long as you are smiling, are not expressing anger, and are showing respect, they will usually reverse their actions and behave correctly. They can use gentle reminders with each other, too. In a discussion about improving their manners, a group of children agreed to give each other reminders by pointing the index finger up while saying "Ahhhhh." After a few humorous attempts at using this technique, they began simply reminding each other verbally, and kindly, not to be rude.

Nonverbal reminders

Not all gentle reminders need to be spoken. Some effective nonverbal techniques for giving gentle reminders are:
- nodding your head
- catching a child's eye from across the room
- smiling as you gently shake your head
- touching gently on the shoulder

Avoid looking or sounding angry and threatening if you want to give children gentle reminders. Such conduct will remind children of the rules but may also encourage defiance, as the message is that you really don't trust or respect them. Your facial expression is very important. Think of your own response to people whose expression is pleasant when they ask something of you as compared with people who look angry or hostile.

DISTRACT TO A POSITIVE MODEL

This is yet another type of reminder. If it is not overused, distracting to a positive model can be extremely effective in helping children learn self-discipline. In nursery school classrooms, when a teacher becomes angry at a child on one side of the room, it is not uncommon for a child on the other side of the room to burst into tears. This can work for you in a positive way: When you praise something one child is doing, a child on the other side of the room, overhearing, may take it as a reminder to change his or her behavior so that it is similar to that of the child who received the praise.

In using this technique, you need to take care not to let the positive comment about one child sound like it is meant to humiliate, criticize, or deride another. The following examples show how this approach can be used much like a gentle reminder to help children opt for appropriate behavior.

Bobby and Jeremy, both age four, are arguing over some puzzles.

TYPICAL RESPONSE	DISTRACTING TO A POSITIVE MODEL
Teacher: *If you boys can't share those puzzles, you just don't need to play with them. Here, give them to me.* (Bobby and Jeremy learn only that the teacher has the power to punish them.)	**Teacher** (to Lucille, age three): *I like the way you're sharing your puzzles with Betty. Sharing is hard to do.* (Bobby and Jeremy, upon hearing this comment, looked at each other.) **Bobby:** *Let's share.* **Jeremy:** *You can have that one.*

Larry, almost four, is painting with tempera. He is pressing too hard with the brush and not getting the paint to flow smoothly.

TYPICAL RESPONSE	DISTRACTING TO A POSITIVE MODEL
Teacher: No, Larry, not that way. Can't you see what you're doing? You're not even painting. You're only ruining the brush. Stop. Here, let me do it for you. Now watch me. (The teacher fails to tell Larry the proper way to use the brush, but succeeds in making him walk away from the easel, totally disinterested.)	Teacher: Oh, Margie, that's good the way you hold your brush so gently and don't press hard. Look how the paint makes such a nice mark when you slowly move the brush across the paper. (Larry glances over at Margie. He dips his brush in paint and starts over, trying not to press hard.) Teacher: Oh, Larry, I see you know how to hold your brush gently, too.

Jack, age three, is having trouble quieting down for a nap.

TYPICAL RESPONSE	DISTRACTING TO A POSITIVE MODEL
Teacher: I told you to put your head down and close your eyes. Don't you see that everyone else is trying to sleep? What's wrong with you today? I don't have time to pay attention just to you. I I have all these other kids. Quiet down now. (pause) Why are you crying? Stop that now, and go to sleep.	Teacher: Let's see, I have a pat on the head for Debby, because she's resting so quietly. I have a pat on the head for Tommy, one for Sammy, one for Justin, one for Cary, and a pat on the head for Susie, too. (pause) And here's a nice pat on the head for Jack, too.

INJECT HUMOR

Humor is one of our greatest natural resources and should be used often with children. The finest teachers I know are people who have an active sense of humor. Too often adults, in appreciating the seriousness of their responsibilities, neglect this important aspect of communication. Children flourish when there is laughter, joy, and lighthearted repartee.

As children develop, they begin to appreciate jokes and riddles and continue to respond to silliness. They often get carried away with mimicry and clowning and let it overwhelm their original good intentions just to get some laughs going. Care needs to be used in balancing the use of humor with normal methods of communication.

In times of crisis or trouble, a note of humor can often alleviate a deteriorating situation and disrupt a pattern of growing tension. Laughter helps relieve tension and promotes a spirit of camaraderie.

In order to use humor and evoke joy, you need to project a cheerful attitude in the first place. Personal problems need to be put aside when you enter the classroom. You can display cheerfulness by your enthusiasm and optimism. You can let the children know, not only by what you say, but by your posture, demeanor, and your movements, that you are happy and enthusiastic about being at school and about being with them.

In using humor, avoid sarcasm. Never belittle anyone, but learn to laugh at yourself and have the children laugh with you. When you learn to laugh at yourself, you are declaring healthy "ownership" of imperfect behavior. Any time you can declare such ownership, it frees other people to admit their own imperfections and even to try to change their behavior. As in all interactions with children, the way we handle and use humor models for them ways they can handle and use it. Most important when injecting humor into a situation is remembering the importance of laughing *with* the children, never *at* them.

Choose your words

In using humor with children, take care not to use certain adjectives jokingly that may not sound so funny when children repeat them to their parents out of context and without your demeanor and expressions. For example, a teacher was heard to say, laughingly and in good-natured repartee with some four-year-olds coming in from the playground, "Come on, you sweaty little ragamuffins. It's time to clean up for lunch." The children laughed and cleaned up quickly and happily. But just think how it would sound if one of the children went home and said, "My teacher called me a sweaty little ragamuffin."

Consider children's individual personalities

It is important to take the differences in children's personalities into consideration when using humor. Some children come from such solemn and serious homes that humor is very foreign to them. If used, it must be introduced gradually and with great gentleness. Such children may respond better to riddles than to outright jokes or kidding.

Some children may come from such economically and emotionally deprived homes that even though everyone about them is laughing, they don't realize that they can join in. These children are used to being out of the mainstream of society. They see without participating and look without wanting because they are accustomed to not getting. Their need for help in developing the ability to laugh and appreciate the funny side of things is great. They can't be forced into such attitudes, but they can be gently introduced to them, given encouragement, and praised for even the slightest hint of a smile.

An especially good learning tool for children who are hesitant about humor is the smile mirror. It permits privacy while allowing for exploration. It should be put in a convenient place, one that is easily accessible to the children. The following are steps for making and using a smile mirror:

1. Mount a small pocket mirror in the center of a nine-by-twelve-inch piece of cardboard.
2. Have the children help you cut out pictures of smiling faces from magazines.
3. Have the children help you paste the pictures onto the cardboard surrounding the mirror. Rubber cement is a good adhesive to use, since you might want to move some of the faces around as the smile mirror develops.

4. Have the children use the smile mirror as a plaything.
5. When appropriate, suggest that a child go get the smile mirror and see how he or she is doing.
6. Make two smile mirrors. A pair of smile mirrors allows children to enjoy this activity together.

Lighthearted phrases

Not everyone is able to deliver humor with ease. If you aren't natural and comfortable with jokes and witty repartee, leave them to others—you can't fake things with children. You may, however, be more at ease injecting humor into everyday situations through the use of lighthearted phrases, as in the following examples:

TYPICAL RESPONSE	LIGHTHEARTED RESPONSE
Everything seems to be going wrong.	Well, look at me, will you? It's just not my day.
No. It's easy to see that's not the way it's goes.	Oh, oh. We goofed that time, didn't we?
Oh, I'm sorry. That's not what I really meant to say. Excuse me. What I really meant was . . .	Oops! I'm silly. I think I said what I didn't mean to say.
Now you just straighten up and listen to me. After all, I'm the one who's in charge and it's about time you understood that.	Hey! Wait just a minute. I'm the teacher around here—I think!
Oh, I forgot all about that. Well, it's too late now. I'll try to remember tomorrow.	Sometimes I think I didn't really get up this morning, because I keep forgetting things. Do you want to touch me to see if I'm really here?
Well, I don't know if those instructions were correct. Let me read them again.	Oh, oh! I wrote it backward. This must be my backward day.

Get up from there. Can't you see everyone is helping but you? Who do you think you are?	*Oh, oh. Are your muscles turning into noodles? I hope not. Come on. We really need your help.*
How dare you laugh at me. Can't you show any respect around here?	*What's so funny? Oh, I didn't realize I still had this clothespin on my sleeve. That's funny, isn't it?*

After all, there's enough seriousness in the world. Some gentle humor and lightheartedness can go a long way to helping us all through normally stress-filled days.

Controlled, caring humor

Very young children have very simple levels of humor. They respond to silliness, mimicry, clowning, and other kinds of simple humor. Great care must be taken not to let such humor be mistaken for ridicule or deteriorate into chaos. On the contrary, controlled, caring humor can be a very productive means of distracting children from a negative situation.

Lily, age three, slipped on some paste and went scooting across the floor on her bottom. When she came to a stop, she bumped the back of her head on the floor.

TYPICAL RESPONSE	INJECTING HUMOR
Teacher (laughing): *Oh, poor Lily. I'm sorry I'm laughing. You looked so funny!* (Lily, of course, cries loudly, her injury compounded by what she interprets as ridicule.)	**Teacher:** *Oh, my goodness. The floor must have moved and hit you in the head. Hey, floor! Stay still! Don't go around hitting children on the head.* (Lily, who has started to cry, is distracted long enough for the teacher to give appropriate aid and comfort without having to cope with a tantrum. In a

minute, Lily is off playing
with her friends.)
Lily (five minutes later,
laughing): *The floor moved!*
(She waits for the teacher
to laugh with her before
going back to playing.)

Ruth and Angie were solving some math problems in a second
grade classroom. John walked by their table and brushed
against it, causing the table to jiggle and the children to
react.
Ruth: Why don't you watch where you're going, John!
Angie: Yeah. Who do you think you are around here?
John: The boss, that's who.

TYPICAL RESPONSE

Teacher: *John, get back to
your seat. And next time
watch where you're going.
I'll show you who's boss
around here—and believe
me, it's not you.*
John: *But I didn't mean to
bump their old table. It was
just an accident.*
Teacher: *Don't you talk back
to me. Sit down and get to
work.* (The three children
get back to their work, but
all are nervous and tense.
John will probably repeat
similar behavior because
the teacher's excitement
reinforces it.)

INJECTING HUMOR

Teacher: *Come on, John,
you know you're not the
boss. I think you're an earthquake. Let's see you shake
yourself all over like an
earthquake.* (John shakes
himself.)
Teacher: *Earthquake's over.
They don't last long, do
they?* (John stops shaking
and goes back to his seat.)
Teacher (to girls): *Aren't you
lucky he wasn't a bigger
earthquake?*
John (returning): *I'm sorry. I
didn't mean to bother you.*
Girls: *We know.*
(A slight note of silliness
keeps a minor incident in
its proper, unimportant
perspective. The teacher
manages to get the three
children back to their work
totally relaxed.)

Jason and Ruben were painting side by side. Jason accidentally put his brush of yellow paint into Ruben's can of
green paint. Ruben shouted, "Dummy! I'm going to mess your
picture."

TYPICAL RESPONSE	INJECTING HUMOR
Teacher (grabbing Ruben's hand): *You'll do no such thing. How dare you. That's not a nice way to act. Now, you know he didn't mean to put his brush in your paint, so you'd better tell him you're sorry you called him a dummy. And don't you ever let me hear you talking like that around here. And Jason, I want you to watch what you're doing. Now you better tell Ruben you're sorry about the paint. Come on, boys, I want to hear you apologize to one another.* **Jason and Ruben** (complete-ly overwhelmed): *I'm sorry, I'm sorry.*	**Teacher:** *Look at that. Now we have two green paint brushes. If you had three hands I could give you another brush and you could paint with three brushes at the same time.* **Ruben** (laughing): *Yeah! And if I had a hundred hands I could paint with a hundred brushes!* **Jason** (also laughing): *And I could use all the brushes.* **Teacher:** *Here's a clean brush for the yellow paint. I like the way you boys have learned to use all the parts of your paper for your pictures.* (By injecting humor into a sim-ple problem, the teacher averts a major crisis. Ruben's anger, though legitimate, is not rein-forced with a lecture about the word "dummy.")

OFFER CHOICES

We are all involved in a continuous process of decision making as we pursue our daily lives. The more opportunity we have to make our own decisions, the greater our personal freedom. Children need help in learning to deal with the ongoing problem of making choices in order to learn to be discriminative. They need help in learning the possible consequences of the choices that are available. They need many opportunities to learn what is appropriate and what is not, what is safe and what is unsafe, what is right and what is wrong, what is wise and what is unwise. We need to help them learn, through training and practice, that they have the capability to make judgments and decisions on their own.

In giving such practice, it is wrong to punish children when they make errors in judgment. Rather, we need to look to our own methods of teaching and reevaluate the way we approach decison making. The essential element in giving children choices is to be sure that all the choices we offer are acceptable. Choices must be offered with sincerity and honesty. Care must be taken that they are really choices and not threats. This is especially important when offering choices is used as a Nondiscipline Discipline technique.

The following are examples of the difference between making threats and allowing children to make choices:

TYPICAL RESPONSE	OFFERING CHOICES
You either pick up those blocks or sit over there in that corner and play by yourself the rest of the day.	*You may pick up the blocks right now or you can come here, let me give you a big hug to show you how much I love you, and then pick up the blocks.*
You sure made a big mess. If you don't pick up those blocks right now, you won't be allowed to play with them again.	*You really used a lot of blocks today, didn't you? I know you'll feel better if you put them away neatly for the next person. Do you want to do it alone or do you want me to help you?*
If you don't put on your sweater, you can't go out today.	*You may put on your sweater. I can button it for you, Miss Mary can do it, or you may button it yourself. Those are really hard buttons to do.*

If you throw one more thing out of your lunch pail, you're going to have to sit inside and not have any lunch.	*You may eat your lunch without throwing parts of it around, you may close your lunch pail and read a book while the others are finishing their lunches, or you may go eat lunch with the two-year-olds.*
If you bump into one more person with that bike, you'll be grounded for a week.	*You may ride the bike carefully without bumping into others, or you may go inside and play with puzzles.*
Stop that humming or else go sit out in the hall.	*You hum nicely, but it is hard to listen to your humming while we're trying to concentrate on our arithmetic. I need to have you stop now, but you can hum a song for us later today either at story time, after recess, or right after lunch. You don't have to decide now. Tell me later which you prefer.*
Stop grabbing those cars from Billy or I won't let you play at all.	*It makes Billy sad when you grab the cars he has. You may share them with him, go read a book, or come over here and play with this clay. (Note: Clay manipulation has a calming influence.)*

Just as important as giving choices is the importance of recognizing that making choices is a skill to be learned; very young children are often unable to make a decision. When faced with several options, they will become confused and indecisive. You may want to institute a program to help children learn how to handle decisions.

A training program for decision making

A training program for decision making should begin with giving children opportunities to make choices about things which affect only them. First on this agenda should be communication with the children's parents. Ask them whether they give their children opportunities to make choices at home. Make a list of simple choices children could start with, such as:

- what color shirt to wear to school
- which of three dresses to wear
- whether to drink milk with breakfast or after breakfast
- whether to have a bedtime story before getting into pajamas or after getting into them, and in bed or out
- which story to read
- whether to color, play with dolls, or help dust
- whether to have an apple, a banana, or an orange
- whether to go to the store with Daddy or help Mommy in the garden
- whether to brush one's teeth before or after getting dressed

Parents frequently are amazed to realize that they have literally been telling their children every single thing to do, allowing no room for decision making. Suggest that they start by offering their children small choices, such as the ones in the list, to help children learn to handle decision making.

Concurrently, you can begin a decision-making program in the classroom. Think ahead about situations in which you can offer children small, simple choices. Whenever possible, try to give children three choices — one choice is no choice at all; two choices can be a dilemma. With only two possibilities, and both of them acceptable, it's really hard to make a decision or to weigh one against the other. With three choices, there is more room for thinking about consequences. The following examples may be helpful:

- You can sit in this chair, in this one over here, or on the floor.

- Here are three books. Which do you want to read?
- It's your turn to paint. You can start with the red or the blue paint or wait for this bright yellow green I'm mixing.
- For snacks today, you may have either an orange, juice and crackers, or a piece of cheese and celery.
- Do you want to paint or do you want to play with the blocks? Or would you rather play on the climbing gym?
- Do you want to play with these alone, with Marianne, or with Susan and Marianne?

Gradually increase the complexity of the choices you offer, but never ridicule children when they have difficulty making a decision. Let them know that you don't want to make the decision for them. You can get this message across by giving them encouragement, saying, "Take your time" or "I can wait while you decide." Acknowledge that you realize that it's sometimes very hard to decide. Then give praise when a choice has been made.

Another step in teaching decision making is to give the children opportunities to select the choices. For example:

- We're going to plant a garden. Here are pictures of several kinds of flowers we can plant. Which ones would you like us to choose?
- Tomorrow we are going to make lunch at school. What are the different kinds of sandwiches we could make? We'll have to decide on just one kind, or maybe we could have two.

Many times we make arbitrary statements which either give no choice or which make the children feel ashamed or inadequate. Here are some examples:

TYPICAL RESPONSE	OFFERING CHOICES
Here's a book to read while you're waiting.	Here are some good books. You may choose one to read while you're waiting.
Stop crying. Big boys don't cry.	It's OK to be angry because your mother left. You may sit on my lap and cry or you may cry on the chair.

or
It's OK to cry when you're unhappy. You may cry softly if you want to or you may cry louder.

Those lines are wide enough on that paper. You don't have to skip lines.

Here's some paper to practice your spelling words, you may write a word on every line or you may skip a space in between.

It's hard for some people to study when you're so noisy. If you don't quiet down I'll send you into the hall to do your work. (The teacher may think this is a choice, but it's more of a threat.)

It makes it difficult for some people to concentrate when others are noisy. You may stay in here and study quietly, or you may study in the hall. Or, if you choose, you may bring your study book to me and I'll find a quiet place away from the others where you can read.

One good way to help develop decision-making skills is to make art and play materials available and set them up so that the children have the freedom to use them in their own ways. Most teachers would say, "Of course I do that." Listed below, however, are comments picked up from teachers during a couple of extensive block-building sessions, in which I'm sure they thought they were giving the children freedom of choice. They started out rightly enough, but then took that freedom away by negative comments and criticism.

TYPICAL RESPONSE	OFFERING CHOICES
Why do you have to make so many small buildings? You can make one big building.	*It looks like you've chosen to build a whole city with lots of different buildings. That looks complicated.*
You always make the same kind of square building. You	*You have really learned to put together that kind of*

could use some other blocks to make towers and bridges.

building quickly, haven't you? You could even choose to make a tower or a bridge if you'd like to.

I don't think you should make a fort. That's for fighting. You should make a nice building or a house.

You chose to make a fort. That's easy to recognize. That's an unusual kind of building to make.

You're making the road too long. There really isn't room in here.

Come and help me move some of these things out of the way. That will give you more room to make your road.

If you don't get off those blocks you can't play with them anymore today.

Brian, you actually made a chair out of the blocks! That's an interesting idea.

I think you need one large block in the corner or the whole thing will fall down.

That's a very complicated building. You certainly know how to work hard. It might be a good idea to check this corner. What do you think will happen if that block falls?

I told you it would fall. You should listen to older people. They can help you do things right. Hey! Don't you kick me! And don't you yell at me like that. If you had listened to me, it wouldn't have fallen down in the first place. I don't know what you're so mad about.

I'm very proud of the way you decided to start right over. I'm sure you can build that kind of building again. You've really learned how to put those blocks together. If you need help, just ask.

Notice that in offering choices, the teacher uses words such as "choose" and "decide." Using these words helps children realize they are involved in the decision-making process.

Teachers frequently fall into the trap of thinking they are allowing children to make choices, when, in fact, they themselves are making all the decisions. The following is a typical example:

Teacher: Boys and girls, Mr. Horace just prepared a garden plot for us near the little palm trees. We have to decide whether we want to plant flowers or food.

Laura: I think we should plant flowers so the room can always look beautiful.

Tom: Yes, and the outside will look beautiful, too.

Teacher: We can plant pumpkins.

Beth: But we can get pumpkins at the store. It's not so easy to get flowers at the store.

Patricia: We could plant lettuce and tomatoes and make our own lunch some day.

Henry: Yeah, and we can have carrots and have our own snacks.

Teacher: Don't you think a pumpkin patch would be nice?

Laura: I think planting lettuce, tomatoes, and carrots is a good idea.

Bob: Then we'd know how to do it, and we could plant vegetables at home, too.

Teacher: Well, I think we should plant pumpkins so we can have our own pumpkins for Halloween.

Mary: But it's not Halloween now.

Teacher: Yes, pumpkins will be nice. They're easy to grow.

Patricia: If we have our own pumpkins, then we can't go for a walk to Mr. Garner's pumpkin patch like we always do.

Teacher: Well I think we've had a very nice discussion, and so it's decided: We'll plant pumpkins.

The children, who had been eager and interested at the beginning of the session suddenly became very quiet.

Teacher: Now we'll have to have some committees. Who wants to be in charge of making sure that all the weeds are out? (No response) OK, Bob, you can be in charge of that committee and Tom and Mary can help you. Now, we need someone in charge of buying the pumpkin seeds. Who would like to volunteer?

Laura: *I want to plant tomatoes.*
Teacher: *All right, Patricia, you be in charge of the buying committee. We'll walk over to the nursery next week and you can tell Mr. Lawson that we want a package of pumpkin seeds. Oh, my goodness, this meeting has taken so long it's already lunchtime. Thank you for helping us have such a good meeting. I like the way you all know how to decide things.*
(Later, in the teacher's lounge)
Teacher: *Oh we had such a good class meeting today. The children are really learning the democratic process. We had a discussion and they decided to plant a pumpkin patch. I'm so glad. I've wanted to have my own pumpkin patch for Halloween ever since I was a little girl.*

Unfortunately, that is exactly what it will be: the teacher's pumpkin patch. She will no doubt see to it that the children participate in its planting, upkeep, and even in its harvesting. But it will only serve as a lesson to them that they are incapable of making and carrying through plans of their own — they must be dependent on an adult.

How much more meaningful this project could have been if the meeting had been conducted in a truly democratic spirit, with all members honestly being included in the decision-making process. It might have gone something like this:

Teacher: *Boys and girls, Mr. Horace just prepared a garden plot for us near the little palm trees. We have to decide what we want to plant. It could be flowers or food. Raise your hand if you want flowers. That's seven. Now raise your hand if you want food. That's seven, too. We'll have to discuss it to see which would be the best for all of us.*
Laura: *I think we should plant flowers so the room can always look beautiful.*
Tom: *Yes, and the outside will look beautiful, too.*
Teacher: *Let's hear from some of you who want to plant food.*
Patricia: *We could plant lettuce and tomatoes and make our lunch some day.*
Henry: *We can have carrots, too, and have our own snacks.*
Laura: *I changed my mind. I think planting lettuce, tomatoes, and carrots is a good idea.*
Teacher: *What do you think about maybe planting pumpkins?*

Patricia: *But we always have so much fun walking to Mr. Garner's pumpkin patch to get pumpkins for Halloween.*
Mary: *He's so nice. I like going there. He likes kids.*
Teacher: *Thank you for reminding me. I had forgotten all about Mr. Garner. We certainly don't need two pumpkin patches for Halloween, do we?*
Bob: *Let's take another vote.*
Teacher: *OK. How many still want flowers? Let's see . . . only three. Well, I guess vegetables are what we'll plant. In fact, we can plant a few flowers around the edge of the garden. How's that?*
Henry: *Can I be in charge of pulling out all the weeds and getting the ground ready? My Dad and I do that at home.*
Teacher: *I'm glad you volunteered for that job. Who wants to be on his committee?*

By listening and giving the children an honest choice without imposing her own will, this teacher has helped these children increase their decision-making skills and grow in their understanding of the democratic process. For these children, small choices will be easier. Giving choices as a means of intervention will also be easier and more easily accepted by them.

Children who have been given choices in early childhood will be more tolerant of one another because they recognize that there are alternative ways of doing things. As they progress in their educational life, they will be skilled in making decisions about what classes to take in higher grades, what kinds of friends to choose, how to dress, and all of the other options that are available to youth today. They won't find it necessary to listen to everyone who claims to be a leader. Rather, because of their experience, they will be better able to discriminate between good leadership and bad; they will know better when to follow, when to choose another option, and when to take the lead.

When there is no choice

Just as important as helping children make choices is helping them to recognize that there are times when you can't give them a choice. You need to be clear and explicit in saying "This is what you're going to do today. Because of the weather, there is no choice. We can only play indoors," or "Some other time you can have a choice. Because it's almost time to go home, I've picked out this short story to read for you." Notice that in telling children there can be no choice, the reason for not giving a choice is also given.

Alternatives:
Communicating
with Children

7

What we say and how we say it are critical in
dealing with children. The ways we communicate
with children, both verbally and nonverbally, are, generally
speaking, under our control and thus can be used as tools for
guidance in the classroom. The three alternatives described in
this chapter concern what we say to children, how we say it, and
how they are likely to respond.

GIVE PRAISE OR COMPLIMENTS

Every human being responds to genuine praise and compliments, which connote respect, admiration, caring, and appreciation. When others reassure us that we are appreciated,
worthwhile, liked, capable, and accomplished, our self-esteem
increases. When we make mistakes, however, we may feel guilty
about not having lived up to our own or others' expectations.
Dwelling on our mistakes can make us feel like failures; the
resulting lowered self-image can foster such behaviors as tension, clumsiness, confusion, aggression, and withdrawal. Dwelling on children's accomplishments, no matter how small, and
giving them recognition and approval affirms their worthiness
and potential and helps them develop serenity in their attitude

toward school, ambition in their attitude toward learning, and determination in their desire to maintain your high regard for them. Children who are constantly criticized may feel that they may as well give up trying, that they have no hope of achieving success and praise. Such children may test—that is, try to prove—their unworthiness by behaving even more badly than they had in the first place; they try to live up to what they feel are parents' or teachers' expectations of them. Misbehavior often increases when such children receive empty praise—praise that tells them how wonderful they are when they know they have disobeyed or failed to meet an expectation.

The following considerations should be taken into account in developing the habit of using praise and giving compliments as an alternative to dictatorial and critical attitudes:

• Praise must be sincere, not condescending. Don't say, "That's a beautiful dress" if you really think it is ugly. You could say, "The color of that dress makes your green eyes seem much greener," which is a positive, honest comment that does not evaluate the dress.

• Praise should be given in as few words as possible. If you say, "Oh, how wonderful! Isn't that great? You really did that very nicely. That was good," the gushiness overwhelms the praise. A simple statement about feelings is easier for the child to accept: "I'm happy about how well you did. You can feel very proud."

• To be meaningful, praise should not be overused. Praise too often repeated loses its value. Concentrate on behavior that shows new steps in growth, development, or learning. Once you've complimented a child for a particular achievement, you don't have to repeat the compliment every time the child repeats the act. For example, if you tell John every day, "You cleaned up your desk today. "I'm so proud of you. You're my best cleaner-upper," John may eventually reply, "You already told me." Tired of being told how proud you are of him, John is just about ready to stop cleaning the desk. A more effective statement might be, "I see that you've finished cleaning your desk, John. You may go out to the playground." The clean desk is duly noted but not praised.

John has already learned that he can please you by cleaning his desk, and it makes him feel proud to be able to do it without reminders.

An exception to this consideration is a child whose self-image is so poor that you need to repeat a compliment many times to be convincing. This, of course, would be a child with special needs, for whom many things would have to be planned differently.

• Praise should not be confused with flattery. Praise is something you give to someone; flattery is something you use to wheedle, trick or coax something out of someone. For example, a teacher might say, "I just love those drawings you made. You're such a good artist. You'll probably be a famous artist when you grow up. Oh, how lovely! Those are so pretty. I just love them," to wheedle the child into offering a drawing. Honest praise is more likely to inspire the child to keep trying to do her best: "Your flower pictures brighten up the day. If you need more paint, let me know."

• Praise should be given for the effort that children make, not for innate intelligence. If you say, "How did you do that so quickly? You're pretty smart. I don't know how you do it," you don't give the child an impetus for future action. But if you say, "I like the way you figured out what you wanted to do and then went right ahead and finished it. That was hard," you give the child encouragement to try other hard tasks.

• Praise should be given for what children do. "It was very helpful to me that you followed the directions so quickly" is preferable to "You're my best boy today."

• Children should be praised for what they may accomplish rather than for what they may acquire. To say, "Oh, what a beautiful doll! You're certainly a lucky little girl," emphasizes the doll. Compare it with this statement, which focuses on the child's good conduct: "I can see by the way you're carrying that doll that you're going to be a good parent."

• Although many tasks require conformity, children should be praised when they display originality and creative thinking. If you say, "You didn't make the tree the way I showed you. I'm very disappointed in you," the children will not enjoy drawing. But if you say, "It's exciting to see how many different kinds of trees you all made," the children will grow with their creativity.

• Praise should always be directed to the persons being praised rather than to others within hearing. To announce to a co-worker: "Aren't they all doing nicely" puts the children in the position of eavesdropping and withholds from them the pleasure of being honestly complimented. If you say to the children, "I'm pleased by the way you are all doing your papers so carefully," their self-esteem gets a boost, and they double their efforts.

• Praise should be given discreetly. Praise should not be an embarrassment to the child you compliment, and it should not imply the inadequacy of others. If you say, "Everyone look. Isn't this a beautiful painting that Joey just made? Isn't he a good artist?" Joey will feel embarrassed and the other children will feel less than adequate. If you say, "Joey, you've balanced the light and dark colors so that they make an interesting design," you give Joey critical insight as well as praise without embarrassing him, and you may inspire others who overhear to experiment with light and dark colors.

Touching children when you give praise

When you praise children, especially those with low self-esteem, touch them gently. A gentle pat on the shoulder or arm when you give a compliment will invoke the feeling of being complimented and convey your approval when you touch the child in the same way in the future. The touch alone will remind them of their capabilities.

Praise for the hard-to-praise child

Stephen, age five, seldom received praise. He was a troubled child who frequently bothered others, ignored the class rules, disobeyed or ignored directions, and was otherwise antagonistic and antisocial. His teacher decided that she would spend one entire day trying to help Stephen conform in such a way that she could give him praise. Her hope was that he would like the positive interaction and continue to act more cooperatively.

Stephen liked books on dinosaurs. One morning, as soon as Stephen entered the classroom, his teacher gave him a new book about prehistoric animals. She also gave him a handful of paper strips.

Teacher: *Stephen, please do me a favor. This book has many pictures of prehistoric animals. But I get them all mixed up. I'd like you to put one of these yellow paper strips on each page that has a picture of a dinosaur on it. I really need your help.*

Intrigued with the illustrations, Stephen attacked the job with gusto. He became absorbed in the assignment and did the job well. Stephen's posture indicated that he sensed he was doing it right. Before he finished, the teacher approached him, and the following conversation ensued:

Teacher (patting Stephen on the shoulder): *I appreciate the hard work you are doing. I didn't realize there were so many pictures of dinosaurs in that book.*

Stephen: *I found all the pictures for you. I know how to read dinosaur. I could use another color paper to put on the pages that tell about them.*

Teacher (again touching Stephen on the shoulder): *That's really a good idea. Thank you for suggesting it. Here are some blue strips.*

Stephen (after working diligently for half an hour): *Here's your book. I did a good job.*

Teacher: *Thank you. You followed the directions exactly right. You may look at that book any time you like. And I'd be proud to have you make some dinosaur pictures for our bulletin board. You can be in charge of that.*

Stephen: *Me?* (He'd never been calmed down long enough to be in charge of anything.)

Teacher: *Yes. I'd be happy if you would do that for me.*

Stephen: *I'm sure glad I came to school today.*

For approximately one hour Stephen was cooperative and pleasant. As he began to slip into his usual ways, the teacher walked quickly to him, gave him a gentle pat on the shoulder and said, "Remembering."

The teacher followed up the day's ego-boosting experience with similar experiences for the next few days. Each day, the carry-over into positive behavior lasted longer and longer. When Stephen did forget, it required merely a touch on the shoulder, a gentle reminder ("Remembering"), and, finally, just a glance from across the room for the teacher to remind him. As his negative behavior occurred less frequently, the teacher began to ignore that behavior completely, giving him more and more compliments during periods of cooperation. At the end of the second week, the teacher knew she had made progress in helping build Stephen's self-esteem when he volunteered to clean up some spilled water.

When you're not used to giving praise

Some teachers have told me that they are not used to giving praise because they have so many poorly behaved children. In such cases, it's a good idea to start out with very simple requests, for which you can thank the children when they comply. For example:

• Say, "Today when we sit down to have our snacks, see if you can lift your chair so quietly that no one will be able to hear you." When the children move their chairs, some will make noise as usual, but some will be very quiet. Thank the whole group by saying, "Thank you. That was much quieter than usual. I'm proud of you."

• Leave a note on the door for the children to read as they enter the room. It might say, "Please walk on tiptoes to your desks today. I'm trying something out." After all the children have arrived, say "I appreciate it that so many of you tiptoed to your desks as my note asked. Thank you. I'm really pleased that you paid attention."

• In the morning, make an announcement: "Today I'm going to see how many of you know how to keep your backs straight while sitting in your chairs." Compliment the children individually and as a group for trying to meet your expectation: "John, you have very good posture. You sit very straight. Mary and Susan are sitting very nicely. So are Tom, Betsy, and Ricardo. I'm proud of all of you. You're learning to have good posture while sitting in your chairs."

Acknowledging feelings of approval

Another way to expand your use of praise in the classroom is to think in terms of feelings. Acknowledgement of feelings, both yours and the children's, is a type of praise that helps children become aware of a kind of acceptance and approval that bears no recriminations or reflection on past actions, but gives them positive feedback on the directions in which they are making positive growth. The use of feelings as a basis for giving praise helps children recognize their power to develop positive patterns of action. Establishing a climate in which such praise is given with sincerity can go a long way toward minimizing the frequency of antisocial behavior.

The following examples show how children can be complimented through the acknowledgement of feelings. Read the first two examples. Then complete the remaining ones.

CHILD'S ACTION	TEACHER'S FEELINGS (RESPONSE)	PRAISE TEACHER CAN GIVE
Suzy gives you a big smile.	Suzy always makes me feel good when she smiles.	*Suzy, your smile always makes me feel good.*
Tommy enters classroom with unusually erect, confident posture.	He's having a good day. He feels good about himself.	*Tommy, you have very nice posture. You look like you're feeling good today.*
Janet brings Billy to you for treatment of a scraped knee.	Janet was concerned for Billy's comfort.	_____ _____ _____ _____

Sherri opens her thermos without help for the first time.	She is capable of helping herself.	_____ _____ _____ _____
Tim gives Bobby half his sandwich when Bobby's falls in the dirt.	Tim is generous.	_____ _____ _____ _____
Larry picks up blocks and puts them away even though the two boys playing with him ran off to play outdoors.	Larry is becoming a very depend-able person.	_____ _____ _____ _____ _____ _____ _____

Praising effort and accomplishment

When you and the children are comfortable with giving and getting praise through acknowledgement of feelings, you can begin to supplement that type of praise with simple statements of fact about particular accomplishments or efforts. The following are examples of statements that convey praise and feelings of approval:

TYPICAL RESPONSE	GIVING PRAISE AND COMPLIMENTS
You missed eight words. I want you to write each of them ten times to help you learn their correct spelling.	*Congratulations. You learned four new words today. You can study four of the words you missed and try to learn those by tomorrow.*
Well, it's about time you re-membered to bring your homework.	*I see you remembered your homework today. Thank you.*
John spilled those. You don't have to pick them up.	*That's very considerate of you to help John pick up the beads.*

When are you ever going to learn to button your own sweater.	*Thank you for putting on your sweater. I'll button it for you, but I'll leave the one on the very bottom. You can try to do that one. I think you'll be able to.*
You better watch your language. Remember our rules about hurting words.	*That's good the way you stopped yourself when you started to say the wrong kind of word. Thank you.*

Nonverbal and indirect praise

Verbal compliments are not the only way of giving praise. There are many nonverbal and indirect methods that can be used to build and reinforce children's good feelings about themselves. It is essential when you give praise or compliments — whether verbal or nonverbal — that you communicate your high estimation of children's actions or potential. To express nonverbal praise:

- Smile approval at a child.
- Nod approval at a child.
- Physically demonstrate your approval of what a child is doing by a squeeze, a hug, a gentle pat on the shoulder, or a soft stroking of the arm.

To express praise indirectly:

- Give a child a leadership task.
- Give a child a very difficult task, knowing that he or she will be able to accomplish it.

OFFER ENCOURAGEMENT

Encouragement is closely related to praise and compliments. Encouraging children is another way of conveying respect to them; it is a way of saying that you appreciate their efforts and that you value them for what they can accomplish at their own levels, not in comparison to others. Encouragement bestows motivation. It gives us renewed energy, faith in ourselves, courage to attempt or continue a difficult task, and independence to reach out for new levels of achievements.

Because our world is filled with uncertainty, even under the most ideal circumstances, children are prone to self-doubt. Our goals should be to promote children's independence of action, self-confidence, and awareness of their own capabilities. We need to think in terms of raising courageous persons who can face the vigorous challenges of a rapidly changing society. Through encouragement we can help children learn to surmount their problems. We can acknowledge the difficulty of a situation and help them learn that, through perseverance, industriousness, and practice, they can overcome obstacles.

In giving encouragement, we can help children set realistic goals for themselves based on their individual capacities and personalities. We can help them learn that to do one's best is a valid goal as long as it is sincere. Such learning will keep children from giving up when things seem to be getting more difficult. They will gradually build their skills in accordance with their growing capabilities, acquiring self-respect and strength of character at the same time.

Encouragement should be based on what you observe to be children's efforts or struggles. It should not be judgmental nor tied in to past failures. Look and see what is going on at the moment and address your comments to that.

Disparaging remarks, sarcasm, and denial make children feel worthless. The children may develop hostile and belligerent attitudes and feel so discouraged that they give up trying to achieve goals. The following examples show how encouragement can be used as a method of discipline and guidance:

TYPICAL RESPONSE	OFFERING ENCOURAGEMENT
Hurry up. Finish that. It's easy. (This is not an honest appraisal of the child's effort.)	*That's very hard. Take your time. Let me know if you need help.* (This acknowledges the difficulty of the

Come on. You can do it. Don just did. (This comment implies that Don is "better.")

task as well as the teacher's belief that the child can succeed.)

That takes a lot of practice. Don had to try many, many times before he could do it. (This gives the child hope that, through practice, she can learn and succeed.)

Everyone else can do it. I don't understand why it's so difficult for you. (This belittling remark implies there is something wrong with the child.)

Many other children are having a difficult time with those problems, too. Just do as many as you can. I know they are very hard, and I appreciate your wanting to try. (This encourages the child to try difficult things.)

Why don't you watch what you're doing when you throw the ball? (This implies the child is stupid.)

Learning to throw balls where you want them to go takes a lot of practice. (This encourages the child to practice.)

That's silly. You don't have to be afraid of a little thing like that. Come on now. I want you to carry that jar for me. (This denies the child's fear and does not help overcome it.)

It's all right to be afraid. Some spiders bite and it's important to be careful. Handle the jar very, very carefully. That's right. (This puts the most positive light possible on the child's handling of fear.)

There's no reason for you not to stand up and tell the entire class. If you don't do it, you'll have to miss recess. (This denies the child's shyness and makes a threat; it does not help overcome a legitimate problem.)

Many people find it difficult to talk to groups. You and Darlene can practice with some small groups, maybe just five or six of us; that will help you get used to it. (This relaxes a shy child's anxieties.)

Well, you got that far; you would be able to finish if you weren't so lazy. (This belittles the child's efforts and character.)

I told you you wouldn't be able to do it. Now see the mess you've made. (This dwells on the child's error and causes humiliation, compounding the problem.)

Here, give me that. I'll put it on for you. (This denies the child independence.)

If you don't tell the truth here in front of everyone, you'll just sit here until you do. (Threats and punishment overwhelm the child and the original problem.)

Now, it's been a whole week since your dog died. Enough of that nonsense. I'm tired of it. (Lack of sympathy shames the child.)

That was hard, wasn't it, to get as far as you did. Just keep plugging away, little by little, and you'll have it all done. (This encourages perseverance.)

That was really too many to carry, but I know you were trying to help. Just pick them up and take them in two trips. There's plenty of time. (This acknowledges failure but also good intentions; it offers a solution to the problem.)

That sweater is hard to put on over your long sleeves, isn't it? Here, I'll show you how to hold the underneath sleeve so you can do it yourself. (Your willingness to help prevents frustration.)

When we make a mistake, it's embarrassing to tell someone about it. If I hold your hand and tell you I really am glad you're in my class, will that make it easier for you to talk to me about taking Marsha's pen? The door is closed and no one else can hear us. (Reassurances encourage a child to talk about a problem.)

I know you're still sad about your dog. You loved him so much. You really need to do your work right now, and maybe later we can talk about the dog again and about how much you miss him. (Your sympathy consoles the child, at least temporarily.)

I don't care how you feel. We're all going and you'll just have to come along. (This denies the importance of the child's own feelings.)

I know you don't like to go on the bus. Sometimes it can be scary. It's all right to be upset about it, but I need you to go with the rest of us. You can sit next to me. I know you can be very brave. (This acknowledges the child's feelings, but encourages his or her cooperation.)

Encouragement, like praise, must be sincere. Don't pretend something is hard when it's not—that says to children that you don't think highly enough of them to be honest, that you think they are incapable and unworthy. Use encouragement to allow children the pleasure of knowing that some things are indeed easy for them to do and the security of knowing that when something is difficult, you will acknowledge the difficulty and provide support or assistance.

As with praise, encouragement need not always be verbalized. A nod, a smile, a touch of the hand, standing nearby— all of these can give children courage to continue a difficult task. Your tone of voice, too, can convey your true feelings, so when giving encouragement, be sure that your voice carries the meaning you are trying to get across.

CLARIFY MESSAGES

Clarifying messages is an important alternative method of discipline. Not only does it mean good communication, but it can prevent misunderstandings. Clarification means that when you request things of children, you do so in clear, precise terms that leave no room for misunderstanding. Compare the following examples:

UNCLEAR MESSAGE	CLEAR MESSAGE
This room is a big mess. (Five minutes later): I said, this room is a big mess. Didn't you hear me? You can just spend your recess time cleaning up the room. (The children were supposed to infer that the teacher expected them to clean up the room. Small children's minds don't work that way. When they didn't respond, the teacher became angry, inflicted punishment, and finally—after all that—told the children to clean up the room.)	*I expect you to pick up the toys and put them where they belong right now. (Five minutes later): You've done a good job of cleaning the room. Thank you.* (Not only did the children know immediately what was expected of them and when it was expected, but, because of their immediate response, they received positive feedback.)

Obtain the children's attention

Before you make any requests, be sure you have the children's attention. You can do this by playing a tone on the piano, turning the lights off and on, or just saying "Boys and girls, look at me." If you fail to get their attention, you'll find yourself repeating requests over and over again. When you become angry enough, your voice will rise to a pitch that will finally get their attention. The children will listen, but you may be so emotional that your effectiveness will be lessened.

Use language the children can understand

Be sure, in making requests, that the children can understand what you are asking. Consider their individual abilities and development. Don't expect three-year-olds to respond with the understanding of five-year-olds. Don't expect fours and fives to respond with the logic of sixes and sevens. Keep your words as simple as possible. State exactly what you want the children to do. Be explicit. If you want them to move their chairs, say so. If you want them to get their sweaters and jackets on, say so. If you want them to listen carefully to what you are saying, tell, them so.

Children must also understand exactly when you expect your request to be acted on. Be specific — use phrases like "right now," "in five minutes" (provided they know what five minutes is), "before lunch," "before you go outdoors," "when the bell rings," and similar explicit statements.

Consider developmental capability

Many times poor response to teachers' requests relates to children's development. Children are often asked to do things, that they have not yet learned. Although many children can learn to tie their shoes before five years of age, it is generally a five-and-a-half-year-old's accomplishment. It takes until approximately three years of age for children to develop good control of their shoulder muscles and the muscles leading from the shoulder to the wrist; it takes another two to two and a half years, (or to about age five and a half) for them to develop good finger control.

Frequently asking children to do things that they are not physically ready to do does not give them appropriate challenges. Instead, it can be discouraging, create poor self-images, and lead to patterns of poor response even when the tasks become easier to accomplish. The teacher must find a balance between what children are already able to accomplish and the next challenging — but attainable — step in growth.

Consider intellectual capacity

Some children may be physically ready for certain tasks, but they may not be ready intellectually. Some children are slower than others in processing information. A child may have a mild learning disability bordering on autism, or even have some strong emotional problem that interferes with the ability to concentrate on what is being said. Teachers who take these kinds of factors into consideration will not always expect an entire class to respond to the same type of communication. Such teachers will make allowances for children who need extra help. They will gear their requests to levels which all the children in the classroom can understand. Or they will give requests individually, as needed, to ensure their being understood and comprehended.

Use consistent wording

Be consistent in the type of wording you use for certain routine or everyday requests. Consistent wording can save a lot of misunderstanding between teachers and the children in their classes. If you develop certain stock phrases, the children will be able to respond to them with relative ease because they will have heard those particular requests over and over again. Using stock phrases for routine tasks can free you to carefully consider exactly how meaningfully you can word requests for nonroutine tasks. Also, consistency gives security to children who live in a world of rapid changes.

Give nonverbal reinforcement

Use body language to reinforce your verbal messages. For example, lean forward slightly to show your interest. This is especially important when dealing with children who have not been accustomed to responding to adult requests. To avoid being defied or ignored by the children, it is important that you look directly at their faces. If you are speaking to an entire group, you might have to first get the attention of the cooperative members of the group and then call the names of those who are not responding. Look at each of them individually, saying, "I'm talking to you, too."

When talking to children who have difficulty responding to requests, touch them gently on their shoulders or arms. This increases their sensory awareness. As their brains receive the touching message, other areas of the brain become more alert, and you are more apt to get an immediate response.

Be patient and understanding

Your patience will help children learn to respond to your requests without arguing or balking. Show the children that you understand that it takes a long time to grow.

Sometimes it may be important to verbally acknowledge children's feelings at the same time you are letting them know your expectations. You might even find it helpful in some situations to express your own feelings about a particular request you are making. (See Offer Encouragement, earlier in this chapter.)

Help children learn the art of clarification

Clarification is a two-way street. While you are improving your own skills in telling children exactly what you want and when, you can improve their skills in doing so, too. Some of their skills will develop as they imitate your modeling, but you can further help them by having them practice giving you messages that state exactly what they want to tell you. Also have them practice including time elements in their requests when appropriate. Saying *when* to do something makes the message even clearer.

You can make up instructive games to play with young children; for example, give the children a garbled message and have them try to clarify it. Older children can play the same kind of game, with the children taking turns making up the garbled messages. For example, "eggs today bought store at I the" means "I bought eggs at the store today," and "ready the o'clock list be ten will at" means "the list will be ready at ten o'clock."

The following are examples of messages that can easily be misunderstood. Read the first two examples. Then make up clear, precise messages to complete the remaining examples.

UNCLEAR MESSAGE	WHAT THE TEACHER WANTS	CLEAR MESSAGE
Everyone get ready if you want to go outdoors. ("Get ready" is not a specific request.)	*I want them to put on their coats and sweaters.*	*Please put your coats and sweaters on so we can go outdoors before it starts to rain.*
Those books don't belong on the floor. (This is a statement, not a request.)	*I want her to pick up the books and put them on the shelf immediately.*	*Please put all of the books back on the shelf right now.*
How dare you. That's not very nice.	*I want her to stop spitting at Tommy right now.*	_____ _____ _____
I'll just wait until everyone is quiet.	*I want everyone to be quiet now.*	_____ _____
People aren't going to like you if you keep acting like that.	*I want her to stop poking Felicia while I'm reading the story.*	_____ _____ _____ _____
You'll have to miss recess if you can't straighten up.	*I want him to stop throwing spitballs around the room now.*	_____ _____ _____ _____
Why don't you grow up?	*I want them to stop climbing on the chairs this minute.*	_____ _____ _____
Well! I'm certainly ashamed of you!	*I don't want him to use vulgar words in the classroom.*	_____ _____ _____
Can't you see you're bothering me?	*I want him to wait until I'm through talking to Gloria before he asks his question.*	_____ _____ _____ _____

Alternatives:
Showing Restraint

8 Have you ever found yourself feeling oblivious to annoying or provocative behavior that usually bothers you? We don't usually think of that kind of attitude shift as being a method of guidance — but it can be. As the adult in the classroom, you can exert a great deal of influence over a child's specific behavior by refusing to respond to it or by responding in a flexible manner. The three alternatives described in this chapter concern exerting control through restraint.

OVERLOOK SMALL ANNOYANCES

The more you monitor someone's behavior and every move, the more mistakes that person is apt to make. In working with young children, it's important to recognize that they need a certain amount of freedom in which to explore their relationships with others, their reactions to the environment, and their methods of expressing nervousness, impatience, boredom, or discontent. It's important to appreciate the struggles of young children as they explore the world of interpersonal relationships and group experience and to find out where they feel most comfortable in that world.

In a group of 12 to 16 four-year-olds, conflict usually erupts on an average of once every five minutes. The children's problems fall into predictable categories:

- I want what you have. (I want to be in control.)
- You can't have what I have. (I want to be in control.)
- I want to do this. (I want to be in control.)
- I don't want to do that. (I want to be in control.)

In other words, they usually have difficulties over sharing toys and materials and agreeing on an activity to pursue.

Children need many opportunities to learn to work these kinds of problems out among themselves if they're to develop appropriate social skills. It's important for teachers to distinguish between behavior that calls for immediate intervention and behavior that is just part of normal developmental exploration of control. Making such a distinction can greatly reduce the number of times the teacher needs to assume the role of police officer during the course of a school day.

When teachers comment on children's behavior, it is generally their intent to change the behavior. But undue attention to behavior often reinforces it. It is better to overlook small annoyances than to blow them up into big ones.

Learn to overlook minor incidents, many of which the children can solve themselves; in other words, don't pick on every little action of the children. Help them, instead, to work gradually toward the achievement of self-control, social skills, and self-esteem. Allow them the privilege of exercising their ideas without constant interference. Ideas and the flow of imagination work hand in hand; they need to be encouraged, not squelched. Too much monitoring of every little thought expressed will squelch future thoughts. Learn to respect the individual uniqueness of the children and to appreciate their varied idiosyncracies.

If you get annoyed frequently

If you find yourself getting annoyed frequently over minor incidents, you might need to examine the curriculum: Is it appropriate? Are the activities which are presented geared to the ages of the children in your classes?

You may need to examine your professional role. Are you in conflict with the basic premise of the program or the philosophy of the school as a whole? Are you getting too many directives from higher-ups? All of these things need to be examined if you find yourself nit-picking and finding fault all day long. Teaching is strenuous and demanding, but it should also be a joyous experience for you; if it isn't, it may be your problem, not the children's.

TYPICAL RESPONSE	OVERLOOKING SMALL ANNOYANCES
Jeremy, why do you have to keep wiping the bottom of the pegs each time you pick one up? They're not dirty. (This doesn't give any credence to the fact that Jeremy is doing a good job with the pegs. It only tells him that, somehow, he's inadequate.)	*You are putting those pegs in exactly the right places. I can give you some harder designs to try.* (This builds encouragement and self-esteem.)
Can't you stop drooling? You have spit all over your chin. Are you a baby or something? (This teacher is reinforcing the drooling habit.)	*Here's a tissue to use on your chin.* (This teacher is being appropriately helpful. He makes a mental note to find out when the child last had a dental checkup.)
Teacher: *I want everyone to form a circle, holding hands. We're going to learn a new circle game that I think will be fun for all of us.* **Harry:** *Not me. Those games are all stupid.* **Teacher:** *I heard that, Harry. I want you to know that everyone will participate in this game. And if you don't like it, that's just too bad. You always have some*	**Teacher:** *I want everyone to form a circle, holding hands. We're going to learn a new circle game that I think will be fun for all of us.* **Harry:** *Not me. Those games are all stupid.* **Teacher:** *I think the circle can take up the space from that desk to this area over here. I like the way you're all joining hands.* (Harry's attitude is not

smart-alecky comment to
make just to get attention,
don't you?
(Harry's belligerent attitude is reinforced by the
teacher, who puts a damp-
er on the cheerful mood
she started out with. The
children all react to her
mood, whereas they would
have largely ignored
Harry's comment.)

reinforced by being given
attention. The mood of
the game period is not
broken.)

DELIBERATELY IGNORE PROVOCATIONS

Deliberately ignoring provocations is an alternative method of discipline that is frequently used in planned programs for extinguishing undesirable behavior in children. Children who are chronic offenders are usually already convinced that the only way they can get attention is through negative actions, aggressive actions, or both. Unfortunately, these children are usually harangued so often that it becomes a way of life for them. They expect to be criticized; when they do not receive attention, they will usually perform in a way that will evoke criticism. They have generally found that it's easier to get attention that way than to perform in a more positive, normal manner. These children are also punished frequently. Thus the very behavior that is being criticized is reinforced, not only by the attention, but by the punishment, which is another type of attention.

In planning to deliberately ignore certain types of behavior you must make certain that someone else doesn't come along and give the attention that you are withholding. In nursery schools, where there are frequently one or more assistants to the teacher in a classroom, there should be some prearranged signal to say that a particular annoying or inappropriate behavior is going to be ignored by the adults. Usually, when you ignore a child's misbehavior, the other children will do so also. Sometimes, however, they may say something such as, "Look at Armando, teacher. See what he's doing?" You must either ignore that comment, or walk over to the child making the comment and use some means to distract the child to another subject. Sometimes it might become necessary to say to children, "We're not paying attention to what Armando is doing right now."

Deliberately ignoring provocations means that you do not give *any* kind of reinforcement. That means:

• You don't say anything to the child.
• You don't look at the child.
• You don't display an emotional reaction to what the child is doing.
• You don't allow your body to become tense because to do so would convey to the child that you are indeed affected by the particular behavior being exhibited.
• You don't talk about it afterwards. (The exception to this is when you want to help a child express inner feelings. Do this only after the behavior has stopped.)
• You ask all other adults present to cooperate in ignoring the behavior.
• You are careful to give the child specific attention during periods of acceptable behavior. Give deserved praise, acknowledgement, and recognition.

Temper tantrums

Temper tantrums are the behavior probably most commonly treated by deliberately ignoring them. Even infants and toddlers learn that throwing a tantrum will get all kinds of attention for them — pleading, loving, hugging, yelling, threatening, begging, shouting, shaking, and even crying — giving them total control over the people engaging in these antics. Adults eventually realize that the best way to stop a tantrum is to stop feeding it. That means giving it not even the smallest bit of attention.

You can help children by totally ignoring their temper tantrums, and, if possible, even their mild displays of temper that don't fall into the tantrum category. Here are a few guidelines that may help you use this alternative to help children control their tempers:

1. Ignore the child, but make yourself available to provide reassurance when the tantrum begins to dwindle.
2. With toddlers, sit on the floor three or four feet away, not looking at the child, but being available if the child comes to you for comfort. If the toddler begins to calm down, you might move a little closer — still not looking, but beginning to establish a bond. Finally, when the tantrum stops, move to the child and give hugs and reassurance.
3. When reassuring a child after a tantrum, avoid referring to what the child did or why the tantrum occurred in the first place. Talk about how the child is feeling right at the time. Say, "You look like you are feeling better," "You look like you need another hug," or "I love you."
4. As soon as possible after a tantrum, distract the child into a busying activity.
5. Try to forget about the incident yourself. It merely was a child's loss of self-control and an attempt to gain control of others as a substitute.
6. One of the problems with ignoring a child who is having a temper tantrum in a classroom is that the other children are watching. When possible, remove the child from the room and close the door, so that there is no audience. When necessary, leave the child in the room and take the audience out. When you remove a child to another area, be sure the area is one in which the child will be safe and can be observed by an adult.

Aggressive actions toward others

When children are acting aggressively towards others, deliberately ignoring the behavior may change it dramatically. When planning to use this technique, alert everyone who will participate in supervising the child. For a child who tends to become very domineering on the playground, hitting and pushing to control others, plan ahead and try the following:

1. Alert your co-workers that this is the day you are going to try to deliberately ignore the child's aggressive and domineering behavior.
2. On the playground, stay close enough to prevent another child from getting badly hurt. If another child is hurt, give very obvious attention to the hurt child and continue to ignore the aggressor.
3. Don't reinforce the aggressive child's actions by talking about them. Don't even mention them.
4. Unobtrusively encourage the other children to steer clear of the bully. Most of them will do this on their own when they see you ignoring the aggressive behavior. Their common sense will tell them that it's OK to not let the aggressor be in control—just as you have done—and that it's safer, too, to stay away.
5. If the bully wants to talk about it, which is usually the case, refuse to do so. Say, "It's all right to be angry with me, but I don't want to discuss your behavior."
6. Don't give in to the impulse to throw in a snide remark such as "because your behavior is ugly."

The following are examples of typical responses to provocative behavior and of such behavior being diminished when it is deliberately ignored:

> Two-year-old Natalie's parents told her teachers that she frequently threw temper tantrums so violent that she eventually threw up. Sure enough, after three weeks in school, Natalie wanted a toy that another child was playing with. When told that she would have to wait her turn, she threw herself on the ground and began screaming, flailing her arms, and kicking her legs. After a few moments she sat up, still screaming and flailing, but watching to see if anyone cared. Eventually, she threw up.

TYPICAL RESPONSE	DELIBERATELY IGNORING PROVOCATIONS
Oh, now look what happened. See, if you didn't cry so hard that wouldn't have	*Sandy, Mary, Georgia, Gary, Sam, Ricardo, Jessie, Ruben—I want you*

happened. Here, let me wipe your face. Now I'll take you over to the table and change your clothes. That's a naughty, naughty girl to cry like that. You know you need to learn to take turns. Everyone does that at school.

all to come over and sit here with me. We'll sing some songs. (The teacher walks to the other side of the room, away from where Natalie is sitting in her vomit. The children come over to the teacher and group around her. Natalie is totally ignored by the children and the two adults in the room. About five minutes later, the teacher goes to Natalie and picks her up without any comment except, "I'll put some dry clothes on you." Five minutes later, Natalie is happily playing with the other children.)

A report of the tantrum was given to Natalie's parents. They were asked to follow up at home by ignoring her tantrums, but giving her a great deal of attention when she was being cooperative.

Three days after her first tantrum at school, Natalie became very angry again and appeared on the verge of throwing a tantrum. The teacher intervened quickly and said, "You're very mad. That's OK. Mad. Mad. Mad. But I love you." She kissed Natalie, who responded with a smile, relaxed, and went happily off playing.

At a conference with the parents two months after Natalie had started school, it was agreed by both the parents and the teachers that Natalie had learned that tantrums would no longer get her the attention she had been used to receiving. She was getting reinforcement for small accomplishments and was responding well. She liked to say, "I'm mad, mad, mad," which was perfectly acceptable. As she expanded her vocabulary, she began to use other words to express her feelings.

Brian, age five, was large for his age. He cried easily and often threw tantrums when he didn't get his own way. The staff discussed the problem and agreed on a plan of action. The next time Brian threw a tantrum, he was carried out of the classroom and left to lie on the floor in the hallway. A teacher sat on a chair nearby, reading a book. He said to Brian, "When you're ready to go back to your room, tell me." The teacher focused his attention on the book so that Brian was honestly ignored. After four such episodes, Brian started controlling his impulse to display his temper in such a manner.

Gloria, age four and a half, came to school on the three days a week that her mother worked. On those days, she got up in the morning saying she didn't want to go to school. She refused to eat breakfast, although she was normally a big eater. She brought her lunch to school but refused to eat that, too. She always sat with the children at lunch time but would not eat a bite of food. She did participate in the school snack time, vigorously eating whatever was being offered on any particular day. At a conference with her mother, it was agreed that she should not be offered any breakfast or lunch, since she didn't eat it anyway.

TYPICAL RESPONSE	DELIBERATELY IGNORING PROVOCATIONS
Mother (at home): Come on, now. You have to eat something. How about a scrambled egg? Or French toast? I can make French toast for you today with that good new jelly you like so well. Come on, Gloria. You need to eat something. Well, all right. Here's a glass of orange juice to have with your vitamins. Oh, my goodness, all this fuss gets me so upset. Now I'm afraid I'll even be late to work. I wish you didn't do this to me every	Mother (at home): Here's some orange juice to swallow your vitamin with. I'll get my purse and we'll be ready to leave. (Later, at school.) Now I have to go to work. Goodbye. Daddy will pick you up at four. (Leaves quickly.) Teacher: You can cry goodbye, or you can smile goodbye or not say goodbye at all. That's a nice smile. Goodbye, mother. (At lunch time, first day.) Gloria, you may go down to

morning. *Come on, let's go. I need to drop you off at school as fast as I can so I won't be late. You must think I like all this fussing and and rushing in the morning.* (Upon arrival at school there is a big scene of the mother trying to leave and Gloria clinging and saying, "I need to kiss you. Please don't leave me. Please, Mommie, please.") **Teacher:** *Come on now. Say goodbye to your mother. Stop that crying. You know you have fun here. You always have fun playing. Stop that and let your mother go. Come here, I'll hold you. There, there, that's my girl.* (Gloria basks in all the sympathy, and her total control of her mother for two hours fortifies her for the oncoming lunch period.) **Gloria** (at lunch time): *I don't have to eat my lunch. I won't eat it. I'm not hungry.* (She sits passively while the children all about her eat.)

Mrs. Cherry's office. Today only the children eating lunch will sit at the lunch table. You may come back to the room at nap time. (Gloria sits in the office in a comfortable adult armchair, her back to the office staff. She remains there quietly for one full hour. Twice she attempts conversation but the adults respond, *"We're very busy. Please don't interrupt."* At lunch time on the second day, Gloria goes willingly to the office, very pleased that she has apparently won her battle —no one is coaxing her to eat lunch. Another child, Johnny, is in the office waiting for his mother, who said she would be late. After half an hour, his mother still hasn't arrived and he is given a snack of crackers with peanut butter and half an apple. Gloria looks expectant, but she isn't offered any.

Gloria: *I've been looking at that peanut butter.*
Mrs. Cherry: *Would you like a lunch like Johnny's?*
(Gloria nods eagerly. She is given the lunch with no comment.)
Gloria: *I was really hungry.*
Mrs. Cherry: *Would you like to bring your breakfast to*

school in the morning and
have breakfast here
with me?
Gloria: Yes. Can I tell the
kids?
Mrs. Cherry: No, because I
don't usually get here that
early, so I can only have
breakfast with you
tomorrow.
Gloria: OK. Will you tell my
mom?
(On the third day, Gloria
arrives at school with her
breakfast and enjoys her
breakfast with Mrs. Cherry.
She then goes happily to
her room. At lunch time,
she again comes into the
office and is given the
same snack as on the pre-
vious day.)
Mrs. Cherry: *Here's another
snack for you, because I
know you get hungry at
lunch time. But after this,
you'll need to bring your own
lunch from home if you want
to eat. Will you do that?*
Gloria: (beaming): *Mommie
makes good lunches.*
(On the fourth day, the pattern having been broken,
Gloria eats breakfast at
home and brings her lunch
box to school. She eats happily with the other children.
Her previous behavior is
never referred to by any of
the adults, although a few

children comment on the fact that Gloria is eating. She continues to come to school happily and relaxed each day and becomes an integral member of her class.)

Josh, age three and a half, had begun to experiment with "toilet talk" in the classroom.

TYPICAL RESPONSE

Josh: *You're a big poo-poo. You're a toilet poo-poo.*
Teacher (loudly): *"Josh! Stop that ugly talk. Those are bad words. You say you're sorry, right now.*
Josh: *I'm sorry, I'm sorry.*
(Five minutes later):
Josh: *You're a poo-poo, poo-poo, poo-poo.*
Teacher: *You terrible boys. Don't let me catch you talking like that anymore!*
(By her overreaction, the teacher ensures that the children now know that they can command her attention by saying "poo-poo." And they will be sure to repeat it because they know she is expecting that they will.)

DELIBERATELY IGNORING PROVOCATIONS

Josh: *You're a big poo-poo. You're a toilet poo-poo.*
Teacher: *I need three children to go out to the patio to ride bikes. Who wants to be first?*
(Five minutes later, three children are riding tricycles, Josh and his friends are playing happily on the big tire, and no one is saying "poo-poo." Josh's experimental language is not reinforced because the teacher deliberately ignores it.)

Sandra, age eight and a half, had a habit, during quiet work periods, of looking around at the other children and making funny faces.

TYPICAL RESPONSE	DELIBERATELY IGNORING PROVOCATIONS
Teacher: *Sandra, this is the third time this week for you. You get right up here with your work and sit in this chair so no one can see those stupid faces you make. You're very annoying, you know. I'll have to have a conference with your mother about this.*	(Before class the teacher speaks to each child individually and asks them to help her ignore Sandra's clowning around. They are all very cooperative. At class time, Sandra is totally ignored by the children and the teacher. After about ten minutes, she turns to her work and pursues it industriously. The pattern is broken and she seldom repeats the behavior after that.)

RECONSIDER THE SITUATION

Reconsidering a decision in front of a child is very difficult for most adults and is really extremely foreign to many teachers. Somehow, we labor under the myth that, once we've set a rule or established a policy, we will lose face if we admit we were wrong and change it in front of children. So potentially gentle, warm, loving, intelligent teachers operate their classrooms from a foundation of stubbornness. They refuse to reconsider any decision once it has been announced to the children.

Yet, nothing is in concrete. Reconsideration can save the day for you many a time, as it often has for me. It might be called *flexibility*. I think I learned its value from my own two children when they were quite young. One evening, in anger, I said, "Just for that you two can't watch television for one whole week." Three days later, I said, "Come quick and see these Scottish dancers. They're really good." My children came to me and reminded me that I had said they couldn't watch television all week. I thought for a moment and then grew just a little within myself. I said, "I was angry and excited when I said that. I apologize. If I wanted to punish you I should have said that you couldn't watch television for just that day, because I'm not angry and excited today. Anyway, I want you to know it's OK for people to change their minds. Sometimes we make decisions in too big a hurry, and that's not fair to anyone. I also want you to know I'm proud of you for reminding me of what I said instead of coming to watch the program without telling me, because I had forgotten about the fight we had."

Yes, it is all right for people to change their minds. Even though one of the basic tenets of sound disciplinary practice of any kind is consistency, it is good to remember that we live in a world of contrasts. The bad makes the good seem better; the sour makes the sweet taste sweeter. Similarly, a program of carefully planned consistency can be stronger and more meaningful if it is tempered with demonstrations of flexibility and reconsideration.

Being consistent does not mean being stiff-necked or walking around with blinders on. It means that you are continuously alert and aware of what everyone is about, you apply rules and use procedures democratically and with consistency, and — because you're aware — you bend or change rules when it makes the most sense or it is appropriate to do so. You use your common sense and change a plan when, after reconsideration, you see difficulties that weren't apparent at first.

In working with young children, we must always remember that we are modeling ways to act. I think it's important to deliberately find some rule or procedure that can be changed from time to time, temporarily, for special occasions, to demonstrate flexibility to the children.

Sometimes we have to think about these things in terms of our own jobs and supervisors. What is the difference between working for someone who is stubborn and strong-willed and who never changes a procedure even when it obviously has gross errors — and working for someone who listens and who is willing to consider reasons for a change, and reverse a decision if the facts warrant it?

Being flexible does not mean that you don't enforce rules or procedures — it is important that you do so very consistently. Rules simply may not be ignored. Every time a particular rule is broken, the person or persons involved should be made aware that it's not all right to do so. However, breaking rules and being flexible about them are two very different things.

Being flexible means that you can say in advance, "I know that the rule is never to use that door except in an emergency. Just today, because we are all so tired, we will lift the rule long enough for us to use that door. That will save a lot of walking. Tomorrow, the rule will again be not to use the door except in an emergency."

Following are examples of other ways in which reconsidering a situation can foster humane, sensible handling of difficulties and conflicts.

It was a rainy day. Larry, four, arrived with his new rain boots on and simply refused to take them off.

TYPICAL RESPONSE	RECONSIDERING THE SITUATION
The rule is that all boots are left under the coat rack, right under your raincoat. It's not proper to wear boots inside. (The teacher removes the boots while Larry cries. He sulks all day, scarcely eats any of his lunch, and upsets many of the other children and the teacher several times.)	*We have a rule that we leave our boots on the floor under our raincoats. But if you're comfortable with these on, I'm going to let you wear them inside just for today. Does anyone else want to wear their boots?* (One other child decides he wants to wear his rain boots, too. After about thirty minutes, both boys go to the hallway, take off their boots, and are happy and cooperative the rest of the day.)

The children have made plaster-of-Paris handprints to take home as gifts for Mother's Day. The actual making of the

handprints was teacher-manipulated, since it had to be done in a precise way. In order to give the children a greater feeling of participation in making their gifts, they were given a number of choices in how they wanted to paint the completed plaster shapes. The teacher made available copper, gold, and silver paints, as well as a number of the usual tempera colors. The children were told they could choose one of the shiny colors or they could use a primary color and trim it with gold or silver paint. The number of choices available was quite challenging to the children and made it difficult for them to make up their minds. Therefore, several children changed their minds after they started.

TYPICAL RESPONSE	RECONSIDERING THE SITUATION
No, you've already chosen a color. I can't let you use another and waste paint. You should learn to make up your mind to begin with.	*That's OK. Sometimes we do change our minds about things. Here, I'll help you see if this color will cover what you already put on.*

or

We don't have very much of that color left. When the others are finished, you can use that color if there's enough.

(In these examples, the teacher demonstrates that it is all right occasionally to change a choice, even though such changes may not always be workable.)

The children were getting ready to go outdoors after a period of rainy weather. The teacher was insisting that the children put on their coats, hats, boots, and other outer clothing. The children were saying, "But it's so warm. We'll be too hot." The teacher said, "A rule is a rule."

TYPICAL RESPONSE	RECONSIDERING THE SITUATION
Children: *It's too hot. I'm sweaty. I don't feel good.*	**Children:** *It's too hot. I'm sweaty. I don't feel good.*

I'm too warm. Please, can I take my coat off?
Teacher: *All right. No more recess time for you. We'll just go back inside as long as you're all so stubborn.*
(The children are punished for reacting to an unusual heat spell.)

I'm too warm. Please, can I take my coat off?
Teacher: *You're right. It really has turned very warm. I'm surprised. Of course you can take your jackets and coats off if you're too warm. If you don't have a long-sleeved shirt on, you might want to go in and get a sweater to wear. It's up to you.*
(This demonstration of flexibility will insure greater cooperation for the teacher at times when she must remain inflexible.)

Alternatives:
Responding to
Inappropriate Behavior

9

The three alternatives discussed in this chapter all address the question "Is the child expressing a need for something through his or her inappropriate behavior?" Pointing out natural and logical consequences provides children with realistic guidelines to help them choose one behavior over another and assess the consequences of their actions. Sometimes they need a little space and quiet time in which to breathe and recover control of their feelings; at other times they simply need some physical and demonstrative reassurance that they are loved and cared for.

POINT OUT NATURAL, OR LOGICAL, CONSEQUENCES

When you adopt Nondiscipline Discipline, you allow children to learn many things through the natural consequences of their own actions. When children adhere to limits and rules and cooperate with others, they are well liked and receive positive feedback through the acceptance and the cooperation of others. They develop an inner awareness that they are doing well and that they are winning approval.

By the same token, when children ignore or overstep limits, there are other kinds of consequences. If they are of preschool age, especially two and three, they may not connect the consequences to their actions. It is important that you clarify for these children the natural consequences of their behavior. The following examples show how this approach can help children modify the way they behave:

TYPICAL RESPONSE	POINTING OUT NATURAL CONSEQUENCES
Bad boy. Don't touch. See what you did now?	*When you touch hot things your hand gets burned.*
See that? People don't like to play with bad boys.	*Tommy doesn't like to be hit. That makes him not want to play with you.*
Well, that serves you right. I told you to drive carefully.	*When you make a short turn with this bike it tips over.*
What a selfish little girl you are. Nobody's going to like you.	*Sally doesn't want to share with you, because she thinks you don't want to share with her.*
I told you to keep that apron on. Now look at you. You should learn to listen. You know we have rules about painting. Wait until your mother sees that.	*Oh, oh. You took your apron off and now you have paint all over your dress. Maybe it will wash out.*

Children do not begin to think logically until they are around six and a half or seven years old. Even then, it takes years of practice to become skilled in the use of logic. Therefore, this alternative will not always be clearly understood by preschool children. Kindergarten children will respond to it some of the time. Elementary school-aged children may respond well and even learn to determine the natural and logical consequences of their own behavior.

Great care must be taken that this alternative does not become a punishment. In the following examples, the tone of voice and demeanor of the teacher pointing out the logical consequences are critical matters.

TYPICAL RESPONSE	POINTING OUT LOGICAL CONSEQUENCES
Well, now look at what you did. You spilled Sheila's thermos. That's why you're supposed to sit still during lunch.	*You can share your milk with Sheila since she doesn't have any now.*
What a sloppy paper. I refuse to grade this mess. You'll just have to do it over. Of course, your grade is already lowered, because it's going to be late now.	*I can't read this. Please do it over.*
You should know better than that. You're spoiling this whole session for everyone. For the next week you can stay at your desk and read during our music times.	*You act as though you don't want to sing with us today, so you may go to your desk and read until we finish.*

Pointing out logical consequences can help children develop the self-discipline that is the goal of the entire Nondiscipline Discipline program. However, logical consequences must definitely be separated from punishment. Your demeanor and other body language, the tone of your voice, and the words you use will tell children whether you are employing a punitive attitude. If you are, then you are reinforcing the wrong behavior, and it will probably happen again. It seems that repeated punishments serve to build up defiance, and misbehavior often will be repeated simply as an unconscious means of retaliation — it's as though the children want to say to you, "I'll show you that, no matter how much you punish me, I'll still be in control."

PROVIDE RENEWAL TIME

Although the term may be new to you, *renewal time* is one of the oldest and most common forms of discipline and is widely used in both homes and schools. It may be most familiar in its punitive forms: "Go to your room," "Go to the office," or "Time out." Used as a means of helping children rather than as a means of punishment, however, it is one of the most effective alternatives to abusive discipline.

I think it matters what you call this special kind of alone time. Time out is a widely used term, but it tends to be overused, as it can be applied to many different kinds of situations. It often characterizes punitive isolation. I prefer the term renewal time. It is easy to say and it means what I really want—a chance for the inner self to become renewed, as opposed to the whole self being "out." Specifying what you really want can help you avoid automatic reactions to punitive discipline.

Explain renewal time to children

It can be helpful to explain to children exactly what renewal time is and what its purpose is when you are discussing classroom rules. Tell the children that you will sometimes use renewal time when they misbehave. Tell them the truth: that it will give them a chance to renew their feelings and will probably give the teacher—and other children who may be involved—a chance to renew their feelings, too. Explain that after renewal time, everyone just starts over.

When misbehavior occurs and you invoke renewal time, try to gear your terminology to the time, the child, and the incident, varying it according to the severity of the misbehavior and the age and personality of the child. Some phrases and directions that I find useful are:
- "Being alone for a little while."
- "Playing quietly over here."
- "I want you to sit over here right now and have a little renewal time. You may read this book. When you're feeling better you can go back to your playing."
- "I want you to sit right here, where no one can bother you, while you have some renewal time." (This saves face for a child who embarrasses easily.)
- "That kind of behavior simply is not allowed in this room. I want you to go sit outside the doorway for some renewal time until you feel more relaxed."

- "You've been having trouble since you got here this morning. I think it would be a good idea for you to go to the office for a while. You can read or color in there."

What I really try to do with such phrases and directions is give children — and teachers — time to renew their spirits, a chance to straighten out mixed-up feelings, and a chance to regain their composure and ease inner tension. I don't always use the words *renewal time*, but I want people I work with to be familiar with them. I phrase this alternative to help children save face. I'm interested in getting them into an emotional condition in which they can be cooperative, rather than punishing them.

Where to go and what to do

There are times when removal from the group should be removal from the room, as well. A school director or principal could provide space in his or her office for children who need renewal time. The teachers on my staff know they can send children to me for renewal time whenever they feel it would be helpful to the children or in the best interest of the class.

Elementary school children can be asked to sit in the hall or in some other adjacent area, since they don't need as close supervision as preschoolers. Even they, however, should not be made to feel totally isolated. They should be in a place where they can see you or some other person in authority, even if from a distance.

In some cases, it can help to move a child to another class for an hour, a day, or even a week. Often such a move can shed light on the source of a specific problem.

In my office there is a small table at which children have a choice of coloring, looking at books, or playing with an old adding machine. Coloring can have a very calming influence. Adults frequently doodle when they are nervous or upset about something or when they're allowing their thoughts to flow. Coloring can have the same beneficial effects on children.

Since the office staff is legitimately busy, children sitting at the table are left alone. It is not a place of punishment. I believe that children already feel bad when they have done wrong. To the misbehaving child, the attitude in the office is, "We all lose control sometimes. We all make mistakes. You are being given a chance to regain your self-control." Renewal time, wherever it takes place, is not a time for extracting meaningless promises, such as "I won't do it again." In fact, talking about the behavior that caused the need for renewal time only reinforces the behavior, since it demonstrates to the child that the behavior leads to one-to-one interaction with an adult.

On the other hand, renewal time is not a time for saying, "You just sit there and think about what you did." When I make a mistake at work, such as billing a client twice or forgetting to call the repair man, I do not want someone to say to me, "You just sit there and think about what you did." Usually I prefer to be by myself for a while to recoup my feelings and my composure. Then I'm ready to take action to rectify whatever it was I did wrong. But I certainly don't want to be commanded to "think about it." When I get embarrassed, I need a cooling-off period. Children do, too.

I seldom tell a child when to return to his or her room. The children seem to sense when they have achieved the purpose of the alone time. After five, ten, or even twenty minutes, they realize that no one is paying any attention to them, and they silently get up and leave. Or they may ask, "May I go back to my room now?" The answer is usually yes.

How long to stay away

The length of time alone must be adjusted for each individual. I've seen teachers effectively remove children from the group for no more than three or four minutes—just long enough to interrupt deteriorating behavior and to give them a chance to take an apparently much needed inner breath. Some children may need fifteen or twenty minutes—or more. I've said to some children, "You really need to be by yourself for a long time. It seems like others are just bothering you too much today." Such a child might need to be alone for as long as half an hour. A tired child will need more time than a rested child. An extremely upset child may need more time than one who does not seem very emotionally excited.

Sometimes the child doesn't really need very much time, but the teacher does. In such cases, if the child is in my office, I offer more books to read and paper on which to draw and say, truthfully, "Your teacher wants you to stay here longer."

Extinguishing a particular misbehavior

Renewal time is an effective method for extinguishing inappropriate behavior. For example, Eddie, age four and a half, had an annoying habit of poking other children in the ribs. He did it over and over again. The children and the different teachers always made a big to-do about it. One day the teacher told Eddie that she didn't want him to do it anymore. "Everytime you poke someone," she said, "you'll have a renewal time."

Several times during the next two-hour period, Eddie was taken quietly by the hand with no comment and led to a chair that had been placed behind the teacher's desk, away from the play areas. There were some books on a chair next to his that he could look at. Nothing else was said to him. After about five minutes the teacher said, "You may go play now." This continued for two days. On the third day, he poked a child only once, and by the fourth day he seemed to have overcome the habit. He was much more relaxed in his play, and seemed to be relieved that he had been helped to rid himself of the habit.

Keep a nonpunitive attitude

Renewal time needs to be used with much care and thoughtfulness to prevent it from becoming a punishment or from reinforcing inappropriate behavior. It should be neutral. If the teacher is really excited and angry, it is all right to say so. But once a child is in an alone place, there should be no overattention and no pretending that the child isn't there. The child should be essentially ignored, but not rejected. The situation should not be unpleasant, but not so pleasant that children will deliberately misbehave in the hopes of having a renewal time. They should be treated humanely, but not so lovingly and tenderly that renewal time becomes a treat. It happens. I witnessed the following incident during my early years as a teacher.

> **Jim, age four, pushed someone off a tricycle within five minutes of arriving at school. I immediately sent him inside and told him to sit down in my office, where I gave him a bowl of nuts and a nutcracker. I said, "I need these for snack time. Please crack them open for me." I showed him how to use the nutcracker, and he went to work on the task. I stepped out into the hallway for a moment. When I came back in, I saw his friend at the door, halfway in the room. "No," Jimmy was saying, "First you have to go hit somebody. Then you can come in."**

The nut-cracking job was really an enjoyable activity for Jimmy. I had reasoned that it would help him use up some of his abundant energy. However, I was obviously reinforcing his coming into the office by my too welcome attitude and support. I quietly removed him from the table at which he was working and said, "I've changed my mind. I need to have you sit over here, away from the window, just looking at this book. No talking, please."

But the damage was done. In subsequent weeks I had to find other ways of dealing with Jimmy to avoid inviting him into the office.

When should renewal time be given?

Renewal time should be invoked at the time of an incident or as soon afterwards as possible. If you can interrupt unacceptable behavior while it is happening by removing the child to another area, the alone time will serve the purpose of stopping the behavior. The time can be short because the emotions will not yet have had a chance to build up. But if you allow a behavior to continue for a time and then decide to intervene by removing one or more children to another area, their emotions will have had time to build up to a higher level. In such cases, some children may need help in calming down before they can handle being alone without it becoming a form of punishment.

The following examples show how renewal time can be used as a response to misbehavior:

Marci, age four and a half, walked over to three other children who were playing in the housekeeping play area. She kicked the doll bed and said, "I'm gonna mess this all up. It's ugly."

TYPICAL RESPONSE	PROVIDING RENEWAL TIME
Marci! (Teacher grabs Marci by her arm and drags her away from the others.) *Marci, when are you going to start acting your age? You'd better sit down over here and think about that. Don't you dare move or talk until I tell you to.*	*Marci, come over to me right now.* (Teacher steps forward to take her hand.) *I'd like you to sit over here and read quietly for a while until you feel better.* (Five minutes later, noticing that Marci seems relaxed, the teacher suggests that she go play.)

Enrique, age five, walked past a table where Cindy, age four and a half, was playing with some manipulative toys. Enrique stopped suddenly, leaned over the table, and messed up the puzzle pieces Cindy had fitted.

TYPICAL RESPONSE	PROVIDING RENEWAL TIME
I saw that! What a terrible way to act. You can't go around doing things like that to people. Five minutes time out for you. You just sit down and be quiet. One more thing like that, and you'll really be sorry. (The teacher does a good job of both belittling and threat-	(Teacher approaches Enrique and talks to him in a low voice.) *You may sit in this chair right here for a few minutes, Enrique. Here's a book to look at. No talking please.* (In this case, Enrique is not told when to get up. He sits quietly for a while, then, feeling

ening Enrique, who has four more time outs in the morning.)

calmed down from whatever it was that upset him, he starts moving about the room, pleasantly. He remains in a good mood for the rest of the morning.)

Donny, almost five, was having a bad day. He had fallen down a couple of times and knocked a pitcher of water off of a table accidentally. He sat down in the center of the room and yelled, "Everybody shut up. Just shut up."

TYPICAL RESPONSE	PROVIDING RENEWAL TIME
You're really being a pest today. You just come with me down to the office. You can stay there until you learn to be a good boy. (Donny is being punished for having a bad day.)	*You're really having a hard time today. Come, let's go down to the office. You can sit there and color some pictures. That will help you relax.* (The teacher is trying to find a way to be helpful to Donny without condoning his behavior.)

Robert, age five, came running in from the playground, laughing. He took a drink of water, filled his mouth with it, and exuberantly spit the water into another child's face.

TYPICAL RESPONSE	PROVIDING RENEWAL TIME
Robert! What do you think you're doing? You get too excited. That's another time out for you. That's the fifth time today. Can't you remember anything? (Robert knew he'd get the time out, but it was such fun to spit the water, he decided to do it anyway.)	*Robert, Paul feels badly when you spit in his face. He doesn't like it. You look like you're very excited. I want you to come over here and play with this clay. It will help you feel better.* (Robert is obviously overstimulated. He really needs an opportunity to calm down. Kneading clay is excellent for this purpose.)

Diana, eight, kept making comments aloud during a quiet study session.

TYPICAL RESPONSE	PROVIDING RENEWAL TIME
Diana, do we have to go through that again? Don't you realize that everyone wants the room to be quiet so they can finish their lessons? I can't have you sitting there making all that noise when you were asked to study quietly. You may go sit out in the hall. I'm so angry I don't know how long you'll have to stay there. (Out in the hall, Diana continues to make comments, until the teacher finally slams the door shut so that the people in the room can't hear her.)	(Teacher walks over to Diana and speaks quietly.) *I want you to finish your work in the hall, please.* (The teacher helps Diana quietly move her desk-chair into the hallway, watches her get started in her work, and returns to her own desk. Diana squirms around a little but quietly finishes her work while the other children do theirs.)

As easy as it is to use as an alternative method of discipline, renewal time is not effective for all children. If you find that the same child is being given renewal time over and over again, it is obviously not serving its purpose. Perhaps the child isn't old enough or intelligent enough to grasp the meaning of the separation from the group. Perhaps the child has experienced so much isolation at home that it has no meaning at school. Perhaps the child's repetitive misbehavior is due to some physical condition that needs to be treated. But for the majority of normal preschool and early elementary age children, this method is effective.

GIVE HUGS AND CARING

Some children are convinced that the only way they can get attention (especially from an adult) is to annoy others. You can give praise and encouragement and even totally ignore problem behavior, but it continues. Sometimes what children need is, not talking or explaining, but just plenty of hugs and caring. The following true story demonstrates the value of open affection in overcoming a child's self-hate.

Becky, nine, was a bright, interesting girl. She was a good actress and good at manipulating adults, especially her parents. She had suffered severe emotional trauma, due to some unfortunate family situations that occurred in her preschool years, which occasionally resurfaced to trouble her again. (Her parents, both professionals, were very cooperative and had sought many means to help this child.) Becky had a penchant for self-mutilation. When she couldn't annoy someone else, she'd frequently pick on herself — actually hurt herself with pins, pinching, and other means.

Becky's teacher patiently helped her along with her academic studies. Often she arranged private places for Becky to do her work so she couldn't disturb others. She used praise, encouragement, reminders, discussions, and most of the other alternatives discussed in this book. She once spent an entire week keeping Becky at her side, having her earn free time. Most of these efforts helped Becky maintain control but eventually Becky would regress to her old behavior.

One day, Becky's teacher decided to try a new approach. She talked to Becky about how she got so worried and upset about things. She said, "I know you want attention. From now on, when I see you getting upset, I'll come and give you a hug." The teacher did this patiently for several days. The minute Becky began to annoy someone, the teacher would go to her and hug her. Four days passed. On the fifth day, Becky started the morning in a fairly good mood and be-haved fairly well during the first hour of the day. Then she began to get restless. The teacher noticed her fidgeting a little and beginning to pick at her skin. Suddenly, Becky got up from her desk, came to the teacher and said, "I need a big hug." This happened four more times that day. On the next day, Becky did not ask for hugs, but they were offered by the teacher. On the seventh school day, Becky again asked for hugs on three different occasions. On the eighth day, the teacher hugged her when she arrived, and Becky sailed through the rest of the day without any big problems, although she was noticed struggling to retain control of herself two or three times.

Five weeks later, although she still had some problems to overcome, Becky was a much happier, more cooperative member of the class, with greater feelings of self-worth and self-esteem.

Alternatives:
Arranging Discussion

10

Once conflict erupts, children and adults need to know how to resolve it without recourse to violence. Teaching children to describe their own emotions and motives, to listen empathetically to what others have to say, and to find common ground on which differences can be resolved are among the most important skills teachers can impart. It is just as important that we use discussion techniques ourselves in settling differences that come up in the classroom.

ARRANGE DISCUSSION AMONG THE CHILDREN

Discussion is a legitimate and positive means of helping children develop social skills. When they have been involved in conflict with you or with other children, when they have been behaving poorly and displaying negative behavior, children can be taught to discuss problems. Discussion can forestall arguments, teach children that disputes can be settled in a nonviolent manner, and provide a vehicle for venting feelings.

To understand the value of helping children learn the art of discussion, picture yourself when you have made a mistake. Do you like being yelled at and berated in front of others? Would you

147

want to be punished by having your pay docked or having your lunch hour privileges taken away for a week? Or would you prefer to be given an opportunity to discuss the situation with whomever else was involved and to establish a plan for appropriate behavior or action to take if a similar situation arises in the future?

So it is with children. Discussion gives them an opportunity to evaluate what took place and to plan an alternative for the next time. It also means that both sides can present their points of view, talk about their feelings, and come to some terms of understanding one another, even though they still may disagree.

What a discussion is not

- A discussion is not an argument or a dispute. In arguments and disputes, everyone talks about what happened and about how they felt or about what they feel is right, but no one listens.
- A discussion is not a one-sided lecture. In one-sided lectures, only one person gets to present a point of view; the others involved do not.
- A discussion is not nagging and rehashing for the purpose of producing guilt, which is merely an alternative to saying, "You had better listen to me. I'm the person with the power."

What a discussion is

- A discussion is when two or more persons present their individual or opposing points of view, along with their feelings about those points of view, while listening carefully to one another.
- A discussion is an opportunity for the parties involved to evaluate what caused the disagreement and to figure out an alternative for the next time the same or a similar situation arises.
- A discussion is a means of helping children learn to solve their own problems with the support of one another.

- A discussion is a way of saying to children, "Your perceptions and feelings are important, even though they may differ from mine."
- A discussion is a way of saying to children that you trust them.

Conversation

Conversation is the first step toward discussion. In the context of this book, conversation means sharing information and ideas without focusing on conflict. Children need to learn the art of conversation from caring adults. Too often our primary communication with young children revolves around giving commands and asking questions. They need practice and encouragement to learn to engage in two-way conversations. The following steps can be taken to help children learn to carry on conversations:

1. Choose subjects that you know the children are interested in. Your interest, if not in the subject, can be in the excitement of the children's growing capabilities as their skills at conversation grow. Look for areas of common interest to talk about, such as what their families (and yours) are going to do during vacation or over a weekend, birthday parties, pets, relatives, the weather, and other topics that touch the lives of both you and the children. Whatever the topic, don't talk down to them. You must converse as equals.

2. Maintain nonjudgmental interest. In carrying on a conversation with young children, it is important to remain nonjudgmental. Don't ridicule their misinterpretation of such things as scientific facts and statistics. Rather, relish their willingness to impart information, and recognize that what they are saying is based on their points of view and their perceptions, not those of the adult world. At the same time, don't be condescending. If there is a blatant error, inquire about where the concept originated without making fun of an immature concept. Realize that, as children develop perceptual skills, they go through various immature stages to gradually more mature levels of comprehension.

3. Avoid asking yes-and-no questions. Questions can be used to teach conversational skills if they are carefully worded to stimulate thought. Learn to pick up on children's comments and ask thought-provoking questions to extend the conversation in the direction they have chosen. When you ask children about their preferences, inquire also into the reasons for those preferences. Do not hesitate to ask for their opinions even when you know you will not agree with them. Disagreements can lead to even more conversation and to the first principles of discussion. Here are some examples of thought-provoking questions to help children learn the art of conversation:

• "You said you were going to get a new dog for your birthday. What do you think the dog will look like? What are you going to teach it to do? What other pets do you have?"
• "Why do you think the sky looks so strange today? Has anyone ever seen it looking like that before?"
• Even very young children can be encouraged to reply with thoughts and ideas rather than just yes-and-no answers. For example, even a three-year-old can be engaged in a conversation such as the following:

Teacher: *What did you have for breakfast? Tell me two things.*
Child: *Mmmmmm, oatmeal. (pause) I had toast.*
Teacher: *You did tell me two things, I had three things. I had orange juice and an egg and coffee. I know you don't drink coffee.*
Child: *Milk.*
Teacher: *What about milk?*
Child: *Drink it. Like it.*

4. Play games like the following to help children become familiar with discussion techniques:
   a. Listening
      Children sit in groups of three and take turns describing their houses to each other. Child A describes a house to child B, B relates the description to C, and C tells it back to A. The children will be surprised how mixed up things get if they don't listen well. Repeat the game with B going first and then with C going first. By the third round, they

may be listening better to avoid making mistakes. Play again with different groupings and different subjects for description.

b. Discussion Story

Tell a story about a discussion you had, leaving blanks for the children to take turns filling in. For example, "Mrs. Jones and I were discussing things to think about when you cross the street. I said that the most important thing was _____. She said, 'No, the most important things is _____.' I said, 'What makes you think that?' She said, '_____.'" And so on with this and other topics.

Discuss problems — don't argue

If you are going to teach children to engage in discussions to settle differences, you first have to make up your mind that you will not argue with them. It takes two to create an argument. Many children come from homes in which arguments are a way of life. These children come to school ready to question the validity of everything you do and to challenge any control that other children may try to exercise. They will try to argue at the slightest provocation. These children are not difficult to spot, and interacting with them will be easier if you let them know right away that you will not be trapped into arguments. You can say, "We can have a discussion about that." Arguing wastes the time and energy of everyone involved. Children recognize this and respond well to being taught how to convert an anger-filled argument into a legitimate discussion.

Help children learn the following rules for discussions. Talk with them about the differences between discussions and quarrels.

1. Listen to each other and look directly at one another when you talk. If there are more than two people involved, everyone should look directly at the person who is speaking. If someone doesn't seem to be listening, the speaker should reach out and touch the person's hand and politely say, "I'm talking to you."

2. State what happened and how you feel. All of the people involved should state what they think happened, how they were feeling at the time, and how they feel about it now. Explaining feelings during a discussion is a more legitimate way of acknowledging emotional reactions than allowing the facts to be overwhelmed by emotions, as they often are in an argument.

3. Empathize with the other person or persons, even though you may hold out for your own point of view. You don't have to agree with the other person or persons, but you do have to grant others the right to express their own opinions, just as you have the right to express yours. Teachers can demonstrate empathetic listening by leaning forward while listening, nodding in response to what someone is saying, and keeping attention focused on the speaker.

Help children to substitute discussion for conflict

If you have established an atmosphere in which children know they are listened to, you can begin having them substitute discussions for conflict. Even with children three and four years of age, take the time to get them to discuss what is happening during a confrontation. Patience and persistence will pay off. It may take weeks of prompting and modeling, but you will finally be able to say to four- and five-year-olds, "Just discuss it," and have them settle their own differences.

As children learn to discuss problems, it is important to let them take the lead in deciding what to say and how to respond. They may still need a little prompting from you. For example, you may need to say:

• "Talk to each other. Tell what happened. Tell how you feel."
• "Listen to each other."
• "Make a plan for what you can do the next time something similar happens."

Gradually, they will carry on fruitful discussions with less and less help.

If the children are going to learn to carry on their own discussions, you must limit any prompting you give to clarifying the rules from time to time. Trust the children to manage by themselves. Don't eavesdrop except to be sure the discussion is going on or to determine that help is needed. Remember that there is no exactly correct approach they should use to express their thoughts and feelings. The important thing is that, with your trust, they will learn to trust themselves and each other to settle differences by talking about them. As their experience grows, you can ignore their discussions more and more.

A caution

Don't follow up a valid discussion among children with a lecture of your own. This would convey to them that, even though they have learned to discuss their problems, they are incapable people and need you to sum things up.

The following are examples of situations in which a teacher fosters problem-solving discussion skills among children. Contrast this approach to the more typical responses adults give, given in the first column.

TYPICAL RESPONSE	ARRANGING DISCUSSION
Phillip: *He took my racer. I was playing with it.* **Greg** (simultaneously): *I had it first. I always take that one as soon as I come to school. I was playing with it.* **Teacher:** *I can't understand you when you're both shouting. You need to keep your voices quieter when you're indoors.* (She is ignoring the problem.) **Phillip:** *But he—he—* **Greg:** *Yeah. And he socked me, too.* **Teacher:** *How many times*	**Phillip:** *He took my racer. I was playing with it.* **Greg** (simultaneously): *I had it first. I always take that one as soon as I come to school. I was playing with it.* **Teacher:** *I don't want to get involved in your argument. I want you two boys to sit right over there and discuss it with each other. Each of you say what happened and say how you are feeling. Don't tell me; tell each other.* (The boys sit down as directed and stare at each*

have I told you not to hit children when you want some-
thing? I'm getting tired of
that. You'd better go sit
down over there and don't
you move until I tell you to.
(The problem is still
ignored.)

other for about one
minute.)
Teacher: It's all right. You
can talk to each other.
Phillip: But you put it down.
I wanted it.
Greg: You didn't have to
hit me.
Phillip: You always get that
racer. I was real mad.
Greg: I was mad too. That
hurt.
Phillip: You hurt me, too.
Greg: Hey, let's go ride bikes.
Phillip: Yeah. I'm sorry I hurt
you. We shouldn't hit.
Greg: C'mon. Let's go.

The teacher who encouraged the above discussion let the
boys work out their problem themselves. Though only four and a
half years old, they were able to tell each other their versions of
what happened and how they felt. It's interesting that only one
child apologized. An adult might have demanded apologies from
both. But the one seemed to suffice for both boys. They were
already liking each other better and were anxious to get back to
their playing. Greg and Phillip each grew that day in terms of
social maturity.

Here is another example of how children utilize discussions:

TYPICAL RESPONSE	ARRANGING DISCUSSION

Teacher: Willie. Come here
this minute. You can't go
around this school hitting
people.
Willie: But he took my tower.
Teacher (not listening):
Never mind that. How
would you like to be hit?
You're just going to have to

Willie: He took my tower.
Teacher: And that made you
angry.
Willie: I was playing with it.
Teacher: I know that. But I
can't let you hit Jimmy. That
hurts him.
Willie: I'm mad.
Teacher: You go tell Jimmy

learn to keep your hands to yourself. Did you hear me?
Willie: But I was playing with that.
Teacher: Don't you talk back to me. Time out for you. You'll just have to learn you can't go around hitting people.

you were playing with the tower. Tell him how mad you are. Ask him why he took it. That way you can discuss it with him. (Willie approaches Jimmy.)
Willie: Why did you take my tower?
Jimmy: Because I needed it.
Willie: I had it first.
Jimmy: Here, take it.
Willie: OK. You can have it in a minute.
Jimmy: Let's make a fire station.
Willie: That's a good idea.

In this example, the teacher fostered discussion by evaluating with the child what had taken place and helping him to state facts. Then she guided him to settle the problem by talking it over with the other child. Even though the discussion between the two boys was very immature and there was no formal resolution, both children listened to one another, felt better, and went on to play cooperatively with one another. When this type of pattern for settling differences is established and practiced over a period of time, children really do begin caring for one another.

Even three-year-olds can be introduced to the use of discussions. In the beginning, they will communicate primarily by just looking at one another. It seems to serve the same purpose as a verbal discussion, and it sets the framework for them to grow into the ability to verbalize with one another, as in this example:

TYPICAL RESPONSE	ARRANGING DISCUSSION
Teacher (grabbing Donna): I see you trying to hit Bruce. That's not being a very nice girl. **Donna:** He hurt me.	**Teacher** (kneeling by Donna and putting his arms around her to hold her arms so that she could not hit out): I can't let you hit

Teacher: *That's no excuse for you to hit someone. Don't you dare let me see you doing that again.*

Bruce, Donna, even though he hit you first. But we can talk about it.
Donna: *He hurt me.*
Teacher: *And that made you unhappy. But I can't let you hit someone.*
(The teacher leads Donna and Bruce to a small rug.)
Teacher: *You two can sit down here and talk about it with each other. (He walks away.)*
Bruce: *What?*
Donna (giggling): *What?*
(They look at each other, giggling.)
Donna: *You can be my friend.*
Bruce: *Let's play.*

Here are some examples of how discussions can be handled with older children:

Two boys had started the day out interacting with each other, doing many things together as if to deliberately annoy the other children and the teacher. Finally, the teacher brought them both to the office, saying, "These boys are determined to get into as much trouble as possible. I just can't seem to handle it. I'd appreciate it if you can take care of it for me." She then leaves.

TYPICAL RESPONSE

Principal: *Well, what do you two have to say about that! You certainly should be ashamed of yourself. Imagine having to be dragged in here for me to talk to you. What do you think your parents would say if I called them right now and told*

ARRANGING DISCUSSION

Principal: *I really don't want to get involved in your problem. You both seem to be having a bad day. I want you to sit down on the floor over there and discuss what's been going on. (They sit down as directed, looking somewhat sheepishly* *them about this? They wouldn't like that very much, would they? I can't understand it. What's gotten into you two lately? OK. I'll tell you what I'm going to do. I want you boys in here every day during recess for the next four weeks. No talking. I want you just to sit here and wait during recess. You can start right now.*

at the principal and at one another.)

Jay: *If we don't throw the books and don't knock the chairs over and don't tease Irma, the teacher won't get mad at us.*

Hillard: *We could listen to her and do what she wants us to do and then maybe it will be quieter and all that. She'll like that.*

Jay: *You shouldn't throw your lunch around the room. (laughing) That was funny. That made me do it.*

Hillard (also laughing): *Yeah. That was a real trick. I guess I won't fool around with my lunches anymore. They sure get mad.*

Principal (approaching boys): *I'm glad to see you boys are really having a good discussion. This might help you: When you feel like getting into trouble, first ask the teacher if what you want to do is OK. If the teacher says no, then don't do it. That way you can keep out of trouble. (The boys nod in agreement and are sent back to their room.)*

Upon returning to their room, they were quite well behaved for the rest of the lunch period. Shortly after class resumed, however, they both began to attract attention again. The teacher just looked at them and said, "Remember!" They needed two or three more reminders that afternoon, to which they responded immediately.

Three kindergarten girls were quarreling. Two of them were playing in the housekeeping area and were not letting a third come in. They started calling each other such things as "ugly," "stupid," and "selfish." The teacher walked over to them.

TYPICAL RESPONSE

Teacher: *You girls should should know better than that! Haven't we talked about being polite to one another? I don't know where you learned to talk like that. You certainly don't hear me talking rudely do you? You know this school is for everyone. I'm the boss around here. I'll decide who can and who cannot play in the playhouse. I want to you clean that mess up right now. None of you may play in the housekeeping area for the rest of this week. That'll teach you to play nicely.*

Lucy (crying): *But they wouldn't let me play.*

Maria: *But we were—*

Teacher: *Don't talk back to me. I don't want to hear your excuses. Just get that mess cleaned up. You too, Annie. Hurry up, I'm watching.* (Teary-eyed and pouting, the three girls nervously begin to put the housekeeping things away, fumbling and dropping things in the process.)

Teacher: *Stop that sniveling*

ARRANGING DISCUSSION

Teacher: *Wow! You girls aren't talking very nicely to each other. You're not even playing nicely. I think you need to go sit down at that table over there and discuss how you can all manage to play together. I want you to be sure that each of you listens to what everyone else has to say. Then, when you have figured it out, you can come back to the playhouse.* (Reluctantly and pouting, the girls go to the table as directed and sit down.)

Lucy: *I wanted to play with you.*

Maria: *But Annie is my friend.*

Lucy: *But I can play, too.*

Annie: *But we were having fun.*

Lucy: *You made me mad.*

Annie: *You always want to be the boss.*

Lucy: *Uh-uh! I just wanted to be the mom.*

Maria: *That's the boss.*

Annie: *You could be the dad.*

Lucy: *I'll invite you to my birthday.*

Annie: *Let's go play we're*

and don't be so careless. I'm watching you.

having a party. (They go back to the housekeeping area and begin planning a mock birthday party. They finish the day with no similar problems.)

PROVIDE DISCUSSION WITH AN ADULT

There are many instances in which it is most appropriate for children to discuss their problems or their behavior with an adult. Usually this is appropriate when only one child is involved in the misconduct. The teacher naturally becomes the logical party to the discussion, and the teacher's mood and demeanor become critical factors in the success or failure of the discussion.

Care must be taken not to allow discussion to become a reinforcement of poor behavior. You should not drop everything you are doing to involve yourself in a three- to five-minute discussion every time a child's conduct is inappropriate. Children would then learn that they need only misbehave to gain total control over you for a period of time. By the same token, angry overreaction to misconduct also reinforces it by creating, among other things, a contest of wills.

Your responsibility, as a teacher desirous of promoting wholesome interpersonal relationships in the classroom, is to weigh carefully every response you make to the inappropriate actions of children. You need to find ways of striking a gentle balance between helping children develop independence of action and helping them develop the inner strength to monitor those actions themselves. You need to remember that you are always modeling behavior they will imitate. The way you handle discussion is the way they will learn to do so.

Not all children respond well to discussion with an adult as a method of intervention. Having direct discussions, however, can help you discover which children need other kinds of intervention as well as what kinds of skills children most need to develop.

Some children, particularly those with serious behavior difficulties, may respond well, and with great relief, to learning to discuss their feelings with you. When you discuss their behavior with children, make sure they do their share of the talking. Make it a true exchange of information. Encourage children to:

1. State what they think happened.
2. Listen to what you think happened.
3. State what they intended to accomplish by their actions.
4. State how they felt.
5. Listen to how you felt.
6. State how they think others might have felt.
7. Contract for some alternative type of behavior in the future that would accomplish their intent by more acceptable means.

When to have the discussion

There shouldn't be any set rules about a waiting time between an incident and a discussion about it. Often, the discussion can be held immediately after an incident, but if the child or the teacher is overwrought, the discussion should wait until the emotions have quieted down. An upset child should probably have some renewal time alone to read a book, color, or do some other independent, sedentary activity. This allows the child's feelings to simmer down and gives the child a chance to do some self-evaluating. After five, ten, or fifteen minutes, you could walk over to the child, pull up a chair and say, "Let's discuss what happened." If the child is still in a heightened emotional state, your first priority should be to help the child calm down. The discussion can wait until a later time. If the child has recovered but *you* are still angry, you should say, "You may go back to what you were doing, and we'll discuss the problem later."

The following examples show ways adults can use discussion with children to help them modify their behavior.

Danny, age four, was very agitated. He didn't want anyone near him. He kicked out at anyone who approached him, but

was careful to miss. He pouted, threw toys down on the ground, and stood with his feet apart and his hands on his hips, looking around as though to see what he could do next. The teacher approached him.

TYPICAL RESPONSE	DISCUSSION WITH AN ADULT
Teacher (grabbing Danny's left arm and shaking it as she speaks): *You can't act like this around here. You pick up those toys right now.* (Danny throws a metal truck across the room, knocks a chair over as he struggles to loosen the teacher's grip on his left arm, and kicks her in the shin.) **Teacher** (grabbing him by both shoulders): *Ouch! How dare you kick me. You just sit right over here*—(sits him down on the chair with great force)—*and don't you let me hear another word out of you.* (Danny throws himself on the floor in a tantrum, screaming loudly.)	**Teacher:** *I can see that you're very upset about something. I'll help you pick these toys up and then we can talk about what's wrong.* (She begins to pick up the toys and, reluctantly, Danny assists. The teacher sits down in a rocking chair and draws Danny to her.) **Teacher:** *Thank you for helping me pick up those things. That makes me feel better. But I can see you're not feeling better, are you?* **Danny:** *I hate this place. I'm going home.* **Teacher:** *Yes, you'll get to go home in about an hour. I'll be glad to go home, too, today, because I'm tired.* **Danny:** *I'm really going home.* **Teacher:** *Yes, you really will soon.* **Danny:** *I think I'll go now. Nobody wants to play with me.* **Teacher:** *I guess I'd want to go home, too, if no one played with me. That would make me feel lonely.* **Danny** (laughing): *You don't play.* **Teacher** (laughing): *Sometimes I do. And I get lonely, too.*

Danny: *You don't get lonely. You got lots of kids.*
Teacher: *You have lots of kids, too. Everyone in the class knows everyone else. We all play together.*
Danny: *Rick wouldn't let me get on the train.*
Teacher: *That made you feel bad.*
Danny: *He's selfish.*
Teacher: *You were angry.*
Danny: *Can I go play now?*
Teacher: *I love you.*
(Danny goes off to the play area, back to his normal self, having had experience in learning the value of discussions.)

Sometimes the teacher needs to be involved in a discussion with two or three children at a time, such as in the example that follows:

TYPICAL RESPONSE	DISCUSSION WITH AN ADULT
Teacher: *Well, what have you boys got to say for yourselves? I understand that you've been doing some very dangerous things out in the playground. I really don't know what to do with you, but I do know one thing: There's no more playground for you until you learn how to behave. I don't know how long that's going to take because it seems that every time I turn around you're in more trouble. It would seem*	Teacher: *Well, it seems you boys have been in some trouble out in the play-ground. I've heard a little about it, but I would like each of you to tell me what really happened. Let's all listen to each other very carefully so we can figure out what to do about it.* Ignacio: *You see, me and Todd were in the tree and Nick started throwing rocks at us.* Nick: *No, they were throw-*

to me that by now you would know that we are just not allowed to let you get away with ignoring the rules of this school. Oh, I'm so angry I don't even know what to say to you. I think you had better get your arithmetic workbooks and I'll give you some assignments to do. (The teacher vents her anger and her own feelings, humiliates the three boys involved, and connects misconduct on the playground with the study of arithmetic. At no point does she help them evaluate the danger that was involved in their actions.)

ing things at me from the tree.

Todd: Yeah, well he wanted to come up in the tree and we told him not to.

Teacher: We have a rule that only one person at a time can be in that tree.

Todd: Well, I was there first and Ignacio followed me.

Ignacio: Because I said I was going to go up the tree and Todd pushed me so that he could get ahead of me. Nick wasn't even there.

Nick: But I thought it was a good idea. So I wanted to go up the tree.

Teacher: But you still haven't told me about the rule of one person at a time.

Nick: I told them that. Then they threw sharp sticks at me.

Todd and Ignacio (simultaneously): He was throwing rocks.

Teacher: What did you think would happen by throwing rocks and sticks?

Todd: I wanted him to go away.

Nick: I was mad. I wanted to get in the tree.

Teacher: But what would throwing rocks do?

Nick: It could hurt.

Todd: Sticks could hurt, too.

Ignacio: He made me mad. We were in the tree first.

Nick: Throwing things is dangerous.

Todd: *Ignacio gets too excited.*
Teacher: *Tell us how you feel, Todd.*
Todd: *I feel that I'm sorry, but rocks can really hurt, too.*
Nick: *The sticks scared me.*
Ignacio: *We could take turns. That's what we always do.*
Teacher: *Taking turns is a good idea.*
Nick: *Can we go play now?*
Teacher: *I need to know what you boys are going to do about remembering the rules.*
Todd: *We can take turns.*
Ignacio: *And don't throw. Rocks can hurt.*
Nick: *And don't throw sticks. Can we go now?*
Teacher: *All of the children will be coming in in about two minutes. You boys may as well stay in here and wait. I appreciate the way you talked things over. Thank you.*

In this example, there was no recrimination or taking of sides by the teacher. Rather, she encouraged the democratic airing of all points of view, encouraged some statements of feelings, and led the boys to develop voluntarily a contract for future behavior. The entire episode was approached as a learning, rather than a punitive, experience.

The regular teacher in a classroom was off for the day. Her assistant was in charge of the class. About an hour after school started, he sent two boys to the office. I asked them what they wanted. They said they had come because they were in trouble. I asked what kind of trouble. They started to explain. I said, "Oh, if it was a fight between the two of you, don't get me involved. You'll have to discuss it with each other." The boys, Chuck and George, were six years old.

TYPICAL RESPONSE

Principal: *Can't you two boys go through one day without getting into trouble? You'd think that with your teacher out for a day you could be helpful to Mr. Dwayne instead of getting into a fight the first thing in the morning. I'm disgusted with you. I think I'll send upstairs for some of your work and you can each sit in here at separate tables and do your work quietly. That will teach you to behave youselves.* (This may teach them that if they fight in the classroom they may have to do their work in the office, but it doesn't teach alternative behavior.)

ARRANGING DISCUSSION

Principal: *Boys, you'll have to sit at this table over here and look at each other and discuss what happened. I want you to say to each other what you each did, why you did it, and how you felt. Then we'll see if you could make plans for doing something else the next time you feel like fighting with each other.* (The two boys look at each other for less than a minute. Then, because they have been taught how to have discussions, they start in.)

George: *You shouldn't have taken the paste. We were still using it.*

Chuck: *Well, I just wanted to borrow it. I was going to put it away for you.*

George: *But we needed it. We had it.*

Chuck: *I needed some paste, too.*

George: *Then you should have asked me.*

Principal: *Be sure to tell each other how you are feeling.*

George: *Well, I'm feeling—*

Principal: *Don't tell me. Tell each other.*

George: *You see, Chuck, I didn't like it when you took the paste.*

Chuck: *You didn't have to hit me.*

George: *I was mad.*

> **Chuck:** *I was only trying to help.*
> **Principal:** *What are you boys going to do the next time someone has something that another person wants? Tell each other.*
> **Chuck:** *I'll ask if I can use it.*
> **George:** *I can share with you.*
> **Chuck:** *And I can share things I have.*

The boys in this situation learned that they can settle arguments verbally and that they can think ahead to avoid having similar disagreements in the future. The responsibility for their behavior was placed with them, but they were not belittled or punished in any way.

Nondiscipline Discipline Problem-Solving Systems

11

Most behavior problems are minor and can be dealt with quickly and informally. However, for children who seem to have an unusual number of problems and for children with known handicaps, a systematic approach to problem solving can be of great benefit. It involves deliberately following a step-by-step procedure, and, if it is to do a real service to the children and the concerned adults — that is, the teachers and parents — it should be done with thoroughness and care.

SYSTEMATIC PROBLEM SOLVING

The system described here is one that I have used successfully, both with teachers and with parents. The primary requirement is honesty. Without total honesty, the process will only serve to create additional problems. Once all the adults involved have determined they can approach the problem with honesty, the following steps should be taken:

1. Identify the problem. No matter what misbehaviors are evidenced, you should attempt to solve only one specific problem at a time. Often, in solving one problem, others will be taken care of. But to begin with, pinpoint only one

problem to analyze for a solution. The following steps will help you in doing so:

   a. On a sheet of paper, write out observable facts only. What have you seen or heard this child do? Are there any accompanying tastes, smells, or tactile sensations that need to be considered? Don't surmise anything. State specific facts, such as "John poked three children sitting near him while I was telling a story to the group. They reacted by wiggling, telling him 'Don't do that,' pushing him away, and moving away from him."

   b. State the feelings you think were involved. You can only assume what others were feeling; you can be more sure of your own feelings. For example, you might state "John appeared to be bored with the story. Tom looked angry. Susan tried to ignore him but she showed her annoyance by squirming and wiggling away from John. Lori looked really angry and disgusted. I felt annoyed at being interrupted, worried at this repetitive and typical behavior of John's, and angry because I haven't been able to find out why John acts the way he does. I think the other children reacted to my annoyance by becoming restless and impatient."

   c. State the problem in as few words as possible on the basis of your answers to items A and B; for example, "John annoys and disrupts the children and myself by poking others during storytime. He appears to be bored."

   d. Determine how often this or a similar situation happens. In our example, the answer would be "It happens three or four times a day—whenever we are sitting together as a group."

2. Narrow down exactly who and what are immediately affected by the problem; for example, "(1) John, (2) myself, (3) all of the children in the class."

3. State what you think is the possible cause of the problem. In our example, possible causes might be as follows:

   a. Genetic: He may not be hearing well.

   b. Developmental or perceptual: He may have difficulty with auditory figure-ground discrimination and thus

may not be able to follow a group story or discussion.
  c. Educational: No.
  d. Cultural: No.
  e. Social environment: He is part of a very large family. It
     may be that he has learned such behavior in order to get
     attention from or away from his siblings. It may be that
     such behavior has been so reinforced by others, both at
     home and at school, that he now does it unconsciously.
  f. Physical environment: He might have some allergies that
     are making it difficult for him to sit still. This may have
     been compounded by overattention to his wiggly be-
     havior in general.
4. Specify the change you want to effect. In the case of John, "I
   want John to be able to participate in a group experience
   without disturbing others."
5. Define limitations to making a change. The purpose of this
   is to eliminate the possibilities of excuses. For example,
   parents may indicate limitations in terms of money, knowledge, time, and the like. Determine whether one or more of
   those limitations will affect the outcome of the problem-
   solving effort. (In our example, no limitations are indicated.)
6. Specify exactly what you need and must do to make the
   change. The following list would apply to John's case:
   a. Time: Try for one month maximum.
   b. Energy: Yours, your co-workers, and John's parents.
   c. Cooperation: By John's parents.
   d. Professional help: Hearing specialist, available at a
      nearby clinic.
   e. Communication: With parents by telephone, personal
      interview, and letters.
   f. More knowledge: About hyperactivity and inattention
      due to allergies, available at a nearby allergy clinic.
   g. Money: The costs of the hearing specialists and the like
      must be considered. The parents may have insurance
      that will cover evaluative tests.
   h. Anticipate the emotional cost of the effort: This method
      of problem solving takes determination, understanding,

persistence, and empathy. Be prepared to discuss the situation with colleagues and with the parents when you need to bolster each other's spirits and resolve.

i. Investigate to determine whether there are other contributing factors: For example, "John's father goes on periodic long business trips. His cousin's father left the mother and never returned. Is John reacting to fears about his father being gone?"

7. Taking the preceding steps into account, design a plan for change.

a. Set up a time table for example:

Week One: Contact parents. Arrange for hearing evaluation. Discuss possible allergies with parents. Evaluate home behavior. Evaluate behavior in father's absence.

Week Two: Visit clinic. Discuss report with parents. Discuss decisions on allergies. Plan for changes according to results of discussion with parents.

Week Three: Implement changes.

Week Four: Evaluate.

b. List people who will be involved in the family and at school. In John's case, the list would include all of John's family, everyone in the classroom, and the school principal or director.

c. List outside people who will be involved — for example, people at the hearing and allergy clinics.

d. Keep a step-by-step record of implementation of the plan. In our example, a record of John's activities at school should include the date and time of any incident.

e. Continually review the record of the plan. Evaluate the results and make modifications as necessary.

PROBLEM SOLVING WITH PARENTS

The following steps enumerate a relatively simple process which I have used successfully for many years with parents. It is almost a self-help system.

1. Meet with the concerned parent or parents. Listen — they will probably mention several problems. Encourage them to pinpoint one specific problem they want to work with — for example, "She won't get dressed in the morning without making a big fuss and getting us all tense."
2. Have parents keep a diary of these episodes for one week. They should list the date, time, facts, and feelings for each incident. Suggest that each day's diary be sealed in an envelope to avoid the temptation of rereading.
3. Hold a second meeting. Open the sealed envelopes. Read each incident aloud to the parents. They will be able to react objectively because of the lapsed time. They will usually say something like, "Oh, I think what I should have done is . . ."; or "That really sounds authoritarian, doesn't it?"; or "I really didn't know what to do next and she knew it, didn't she?"
4. Make a specific plan for changing behavior. An effective question is "What can you do to let her know that you are in control?" Help make a list of several methods. Allow the parents to decide which one to use. Example of methods are:

• Use anticipation: Prepare her clothes the night before. Tell her that they are what she will wear and that it will not be discussed any further.

• Give gentle reminders — gerunds: In the morning say, "Getting dressed right now. Letting me help you. Not fighting me." Clarify the message: Say, "This is what you're going to wear. I don't want to talk about it."

• Deliberately ignore provocation: If, as usual, she refuses to get dressed and screams and cries, say nothing. If she asks for breakfast, give it to her. Make no comments about her being in her pajamas. When it is time to go to school, pick her up, wrap her in a blanket, put her clothes in a bag, and take them to school. Give the clothes and the child to the teacher. Make no comment about the clothes. Kiss her goodbye and leave. (Assure parents that this method works. Most children will come like that only once; some will do it two or three times and then start dressing willingly at home. In the meantime, tantrums and other misbehavior over dressing are greatly reduced, if not eliminated.)

• Offer choices: For example, say, "You may get dressed before breakfast, you may get dressed after breakfast, or you may get dressed at school." (Most children will choose after breakfast but before school. If the child still won't do so after breakfast, make sure the parents know that *they* will have to make the choice.)

When the misbehavior has been changed, the parents will realize that it was due to their own changed approaches. They will be ready to receive help for the next change to make or to make the changes on their own. Remind them of the importance of tackling just one problem at a time. Each solved problem lessens the severity of other problems.

PARENT EDUCATION

The more you can enlist parents' cooperation in implementing the suggestions in this book, the more valuable your own nondisciplinary attitudes will become for the children with whom you are involved. You may want to use this book as a basis for a parent-education program. Such a program might involve weekly, biweekly, or monthly meetings. Since many families consist of only one parent or of two who both work, it is often difficult for parents to attend meetings; you need to be creative in scheduling meeting times. For night meetings, it is advisable to provide child care.

I have found that when I make a title for the meeting that refers specifically to discipline, parents will almost always find a way to come. Two titles that I have used successfully are "Please Don't Sit on the Kids: A Series of Meetings on Whether or Not to Spank and, If Not, Why Not" and "Whining, Crying, and Other Annoyances."

In using this book for a parent program, remember that the alternatives in the magic list are as effective in the home as in the school. You and the parents can work together to develop examples that reflect home situations rather than the school situations given in this book.

THE REPLY

Dear Child,

Sometimes, being a grownup, I do forget how little you are and that you have your own feelings and emotions just like I do. I know you don't want to do things that are against the rules. But when you do, sometimes I get angry and forget that my job is to help you learn about things that will help you remember those rules. Besides, I shouldn't assume that you know or can remember *all* the rules *all* the time.

I'm very flattered that you want to be like me. What I want, however, is for you to just go on being you, because that is the best kind of person you can be. Because I want to be your friend as well as your teacher, I'll try to help you to understand yourself and to remember the rules and to learn about the many things there are in life to learn. But also because I am your friend, when you start forgetting things I won't get angry. Maybe I'll just give you a gentle reminder — just a look or a word along with a smile. Or maybe when I see you getting nervous or emotional, I'll try to help you talk about your feelings. I'll try to help you get them under control by understanding them, so you don't let the feelings control you.

Thank you for reminding me of my own humaneness and my responsibilities. Yes, I'll take your hand and walk with you. I'm proud to be your friend and I do love you. Yes, we'll keep on being friends and together we'll grow.

Teacher

A Selected Bibliography

You may find the following books helpful for further pursuit of some of the questions raised in this book.

Ayres, A. Jean. *Sensory Integration and Learning Disorders.* Los Angeles: Western Psychological Services, 1977. A technical book for the teacher who wants to begin studying neurobehavioral theory and the relationship of sensory integration to learning disorders and thus to behavior.

Baruch, Dorothy W. *New Ways in Discipline.* New York: McGraw Hill, 1949. An early book on humanistic discipline, it emphasizes the legitimacy of allowing children the privilege of expressing true feelings.

Bessell, Harold, and Thomas P. Kelly, Jr. *The Parent Book: The Holistic Program for Raising the Emotionally Mature Child.* San Diego: Psych/Graphic Publishers, 1977. An excellent guide to the emotional development of children and how the emotions can be responded to constructively to minimize conflict between parents and their children.

Bigner, Jerry J. *Parent Child Relationships.* New York: The Macmillan Company, 1979. How children affect what their parents do and how parents affect what their children do. An excellent study in the dynamics of interpersonal relationships within the home, the principles of which can be extended into the classroom.

Cherry, Clare. *Creative Movement for the Developing Child: A Handbook for Non-Musicians.* Belmont, Ca.: Pitman Learning, Inc. (formerly Fearon Pitman Publishers), 1971. A very basic introduction to the perceptual-motor development of children and to sensory-motor integrative activities.

—————. *Think of Something Quiet: A Guide to Serenity in the Classroom.* Belmont, Ca.: Pitman Learning, Inc., 1981. Suggests that the establishment of a humanistic program built around an environment and curriculum geared towards stress reduction can reduce the frequency of conflict between children and their teachers.

Cooperative Parents' Group of Palisades Pre-School Division and Mothers' and Children's Educational Foundation, Inc. *The Challenge of Children.* New York: Whiteside, Inc., & William Morrow & Company, 1957. An inspirational book which emphasizes responsibility on the part of both parents and children—a responsibility strongly based on self-awareness, willingness to grow, and a clear knowledge of what a child is and what, with love, the child may become.

Dodson, Fitzhugh. *How to Discipline —with Love*. New York: New American Library, 1978. This book presents discipline as teaching. Taking the age of the child into account, Dodson stresses that there can be no overall formula for teaching desirable behavior but rather a wide variety of flexible, practical strategies to draw from according to each individual situation — a humane approach that stresses the importance of love and rapport as an ongoing element of interpersonal relationships with children.

Dreikurs, Rudolf, M.D. *Coping with Children's Misbehavior: A Parent's Guide*. New York: Hawthorne Publishers, 1972. This book stresses the importance of investigating the reasons behind children's misbehavior.

_____, and Vicki Soltz. *Children: The Challenge*. New York: Hawthorn Publishers, 1964. This book is based on Dreikurs's system of natural consequences in dealing with discipline.

Faber, Adele, and Elaine Mazlish. *How to Talk so Kids Will Listen and Listen so Kids Will Talk*. New York: Rawson, Wade Publishers, Inc., 1980. This book emphasizes the differences between helpful and unhelpful methods of communication, geared towards the reduction of conflicts and tensions between parents and their children. Principles can easily be applied to teacher-child interactions.

Fraiberg, Selma. *The Magic Years*. New York: Charles Scribner's Sons, 1959. Fraiberg suggests gearing disciplinary practices to the understanding of what can be expected of children at their various levels of maturity. She feels that, rather than punishment, children need help, understanding, and a great deal of emotional support. This book is especially valuable for the understanding of the needs of infants and toddlers as they try to master their environment.

Ginott, Haim. *Between Parents and Child: New Solutions to Old Problems*. New York: The Macmillan Company, 1965. (Also Avon paperback.) Ginott writes about communication between parents and their children, giving guidelines to conveyance of self-respect and positive feelings even when giving statements of advice, correction, or instruction. He emphasizes the validity of reflecting children's feelings.

_____. *Teacher and Child: A Book for Parents and Teachers*. New York: The Macmillan Company, 1972. (Also Avon paperback.) Illustrates practical ways of dealing with problems of communication and conflict with children, for both teachers and parents. Deals with the maintenance of a wholesome emotional climate for learning that can bolster the self-esteem of children and a mutuality of respect between children and adults.

Gordon, Thomas. *Parent Effectiveness Training: The Tested New Way to Raise Responsible Children*. New York: Peter H. Wyden, Inc., 1970. (Also available in paperback.) Addresses the importance of humanistic attitudes when dealing with family conflicts, utilizing the communication of feelings to solve problems.

_____. *Teacher Effectiveness Training*. New York: Peter H. Wyden, Inc., 1979. (Also available in paperback.) This book extends Gordon's humanistic approach to resolving conflict with children by emphasis on the communication of feelings in ways that increase the self-esteem of both the children and their teachers.

Kephart, Newell C. *The Slow Learner in the Classroom.* Columbus, Ohio: Charles E. Merrill Books, Inc., 1960. An introduction to classroom activities for the elementary school child based on perceptual-motor development and its relationship to learning and, thus, to child behavior.

Klein, Carole. *How It Feels to Be a Child.* New York: Harper & Row, Publishers, 1975. Dispels the myth of an always happy childhood and opens doors to understanding the fears, anxieties, loneliness, and other problems of children's inner feelings.

Kliman, G. *Psychological Emergencies of Childhood.* New York: Grune & Stratton, 1968. To promote the understanding of the feelings of children, this book focuses on children's reactions to crisis situations.

National Education Association. *Discipline in the Classroom.* Revised edition. Washington, D.C.: N.E.A., 1974. This book consists of a collection of articles which reflect a broad spectrum in their approach to discipline and the teaching process. Largely geared towards older children and widely differing in approaches, the general consensus leans heavily towards the importance of both presenting a meaningful curriculum and motivating individual children.

————. *Discipline and Learning: An Inquiry into Student-Teacher Relationships.* Revised edition. Washington, D.C.: N.E.A., 1977. A collection of articles on discipline as seen by differing professionals, including teachers, administrators, counselors, psychologists, a school board member, and an attorney. Their varying approaches and recommendations provide an excellent overview of policies that help direct the course of schools today.

Peairs, Lillian, and Richard H. Peairs. *What Every Child Needs.* New York: Harper & Row, 1974. An excellent book for parents who are seeking to raise emotionally healthy children. Contains excellent chapters on anger and hostility and on keys to better discipline. A helpful book for teachers, too, and for teenage brothers and sisters of younger children.

Pearson, Craig. *Resolving Classroom Conflict.* Palo Alto, California: Learning Handbooks (Education Today Company), 1977. This book offers suggestions, insights, and experiences that are geared toward increasing the cooperation, communication, and awareness in the classroom as a means to decreasing the incidence of classroom conflict between students and between teachers and students.

Schrag, Peter, and Diane Divoky. *The Myth of the Hyperactive Child and Other Means of Child Control.* New York: Pantheon Books, 1975. (Also available in Dell paperback.) This is an important study of the dehumanization of child control in the name of drugs, Skinnerian reinforcement, and the world of technology.

Index